DRUNK FOLK STORIES

www.beansontoastmusic.com

For you

GLASTONBURY

If this book is going to start anywhere, then it should start at Glastonbury. My first ever Glastonbury Festival. It was 1997 and I was 16 years old. I got a ticket from a girl who lived at the bottom of my road called Crystal Graham. At the time, I lived in the house I grew up in - Medley Road, Rayne, Braintree, Essex - a semi-detached house with three cars on the drive. Mum worked at a swimming pool and Dad on a building site. It was a bog-standard part of English suburbia and life was pretty normal for a 16-year-old in Essex in the '90s. Computer games at your mate's house, smoking cheap hash from plastic bottles down the park, listening to Nirvana, long hair, ripped jeans, and after school detentions.

Back then, Glastonbury didn't get anywhere near the amount of media coverage it does now. It was still a massive deal but it wasn't all over the TV and what not. It had an element of mystery about it. I'd heard about it through stories or band interviews in music magazines. From the little that I did know, I was fascinated and had my heart set on going. It was our final year of school and summer was drawing nearer. When Radiohead announced their headline slot, that was it. Me and a bunch of mates got together and made a plan to head down. As the reality of the event drew closer, my mates dropped out, one by one, until there was nobody that wanted to come with me. Nevertheless, I had to go. I had a rendezvous with Mary Fairy.

1

I'd met Mary a few weeks earlier at a Placebo gig in Cambridge and we snogged. Snogged is a horrible word that I haven't used for years but that's definitely what we called it back then, so that's the correct term. My encounter with Mary had been brief but brilliant. She was pretty, excitable and she actually dressed like a fairy. I was into her. She'd told me she was going to Glastonbury. She'd been going since she was young and knew it well and, so, we arranged to meet. Back before mobile phones, it was a pretty common practice to arrange meeting spots. It sounds odd now but we didn't even trade landline numbers. She just said 6pm, Thursday, The Tiny Tea Tent. So, even after my mates had pulled out, I still had every intention of going. I found out Crystal had a ticket which she was willing to sell, and I managed to blag a ride down with Ed from the band Planet Empathy.

Planet Empathy were the first real band I ever encountered – 'real' in the sense that they played gigs. My first ever live gig was watching them at The Army and Navy in Chelmsford. But, they're also 'real' because I knew them from around town. They were a fair bit older – probably in their early twenties at the time and I thought they were amazing. They wrote their own songs, they looked like a band, and they were from Braintree. Due to my sheer enthusiasm (and the fact that I normally had a few spliffs' worth of hash), they used to let me hang around at their rehearsals, which were in the basement of Lake and Elliot's - a social club on the edge of town. It turned out that Ed, the guitarist, was heading down to Glastonbury with his new girlfriend and for a bit of petrol money, I could catch a ride.

We left on the morning of Saturday 21st June to celebrate something called "Summer Solstice" on something called a "Tor". None of that meant anything to me but I was just happy to have a ride and went along presuming that was how it was done. I borrowed a one-man tent (thanks Dave), packed a few changes

2

of clothes, took the one hundred and fifty pounds I had to my name, and off we all went...

... a week early.

A long drive, some traffic, and a bit of car trouble, meant that we didn't arrive into Glastonbury town until late that evening. It turned out that Summer Solstice was an ancient celebration of the longest day of the year, and that the celebration generally happens with the sunrise. By the time we got there, the sun had set so we missed that. As I didn't know what I'd missed anyway, I didn't give a shit. I had learnt a few things on the ride down, though. One was that the plan was to camp at the bottom of the Tor (it's a big hill - don't you know?) in Glastonbury town for five nights and then head down to the actual festival (down the road in Pilton) on Thursday. Great. The other thing I learnt was that Ed and his girlfriend were very much in the honeymoon period of their relationship. They'd just met and were quickly falling in love. In fact, the trip was going to be a bit like a honeymoon for them and, although they didn't actually say it, it didn't take me long to realise that they probably weren't going to want a sixteen-year-old hanging around the whole time. I decided to make it clear that I was just hitching a ride and that I'd be out of their hair as soon as possible.

I went on to learn a few other life lessons, too – like don't camp at the bottom of a massive fucking hill. Especially if you've got the oldest, flimsiest tent on the campsite, and especially not if it's going to piss it down for five days.

That said, I had a great time camping in the rain in Glastonbury town. I idled the days away at a hippy cafe, hung out with the buskers, and spent the evenings in the pub. It was great. However, by the end of the five days, I'd spent every penny of the only one hundred and fifty pounds I had, and I'd lost my tent. It literally washed away, never to be seen again (sorry Dave). Still, I didn't let it break my stride. I still had a lift to the festival with Ed and I still had a rendezvous with Mary Fairy.

It was Thursday and we headed down to the festival. There was five pound weekend parking in most of the fields surrounding the site so we parked up there to avoid sitting in a traffic jam. I didn't want to miss my rendezvous, and time was getting on, so I split from Ed and his lady. Ideally we'd bump into each other inside, but if not, we agreed to meet on Monday at the car to drive back to Essex. I grabbed my little bag with some wet clothes in it and off I went: no cash, no tent, all smiles.

As I arrived at the main gate, people were being filtered through into single file and handing in their tickets. It was then I realised that my ticket was at the very bottom of my bag. Not wanting to lose my place, and not wanting to hold up the queue, I starting rustling around with one hand, while walking in single file. I had my head down and wasn't really paying attention. When I looked up, I still hadn't found my ticket but I was handed a plastic bag. I could tell it was a kind of line-up/goodie bag - a welcome to the festival kind of thing. Still not wanting to hold the queue up, I kept on walking, but after the giving of the carrier bag, the queue dispersed in all manor of different directions. Ahead of me was an open field and beyond that was a campsite, and beyond that a festival - a festival as far as the eye could see. It looked like wonderful, colourful chaos. I stood there, taking it all in and feeling the excitement building inside. Then I realised, I hadn't handed my ticket in. It was still in my bag and I was already in the festival! I considered my options and headed back to the gate. I asked one of the stewards how I could leave the festival and get back in afterwards. She informed me that you could get an ultra violet stamp on your way out and they'd check it on the way in. Easy. I got myself stamped up and headed back onto the main road to try and sell my ticket. After a bit of haggling, and bit

4

of farting around, I managed to sell my ticket to a tout for fifty pounds (the same price I'd paid Crystal for it). I headed back to the gate, showed my stamp, and I was in. Entering the festival for the second time, I had the same feelings of wonder. I looked out at the huge festival and an incredible wave of excitement hit me. I was there. I'd made it and I had fifty pounds! The anticipation of the next four days was out of this world, anything could happen. All I needed to do was find The Tiny Tea Tent.

Walking into the festival, I asked the person standing next to me "You know where The Tiny Tea Tent is, my man?"

He smiled and said "Needle in a haystack."

That was the first festival I'd ever been to but it wasn't really my first festival experience. The previous summer I'd answered an ad in the local paper about cash-in-hand litter picking in the Chelmsford area. I was short of cash and on school holiday. Me and a few friends all applied and were told to go to Hyland Park on the Monday morning. In short, we would be clearing up after an event called V Festival. My first festival experience was seeing the absolute shit-tip that a site is left in afterwards. It wasn't pretty then and it's not pretty now. But after a weekend of picking up crap left behind by Pulp fans, I decided that the next festival I went to, I'd make it whilst it was in full swing, not the day after it had finished.

Glastonbury was my first time seeing something like that in full swing, and boy can Glastonbury swing. I'd never seen or heard anything like it. There were people everywhere, music everywhere, magic everywhere. It was incredibly chaotic but, at the same time, it had an incredible flow and feeling to it. It felt safe and dangerous, mystical and modern. It was a huge high. It's hard to explain without using all the cheesy words but it was buzzing. It had a vibe... it was fucking Glastonbury. Oh, and it was raining. I don't want to keep going on about the weather but whilst everything that I've just told you was happening, it was raining. Absolutely pissing it down. Torrential rain. With the rain, comes Glastonbury's closest ally: mud. It was really fucking muddy. But, whatever, I was cool with it.

I still hadn't a clue about the sheer size of the beast. I'd just been walking forward, following the flow, looking for The Tiny Tea Tent. Nobody had any idea where it was but everybody that I asked treated me like an old friend. The interaction with strangers was different to anything I'd ever witnessed before. It was like an open conversation between everyone in earshot. Everybody talked to everyone, cracking jokes and having a laugh. It was as if, on arrival, everybody had let their guard down. We were all there together and the main purpose of our whole existence was to have a good time. It was amazing. Nobody knew where The Tiny Tea Tent was, though, and I was just starting to work out that Glastonbury is fucking huge.

Amongst all the walking, the searching, and the roaming banter, my very real predicament started to dawn on me. I had no way of getting in touch with Ed until Monday afternoon. I had no tent and I had no idea where The Tiny Tea Tent was – shit – I had no idea where I was! It was still hammering it down. Things could actually start to go tits up pretty quickly. I looked at the time and realised it was 6:15. SHIT. I was late. I was just about to start worrying about the whole situation when BOOM - Mary Fairy jumped in front of me. "You came," she said and gave me a huge fairy hug.

Whilst hugging her, I looked up to see a small, colourful wooden sign…. The Tiny Tea Tent. Yes, Glastonbury. Fucking yes! Thank you!

Mary was beautiful; she had big, curly blonde hair, a warm, loving smile, piercing blue eyes and wings. She actually had wings. She also seemed extremely pleased to see me. We hugged again and my new predicament dawned on me. How the hell was I going to explain to Mary that I had no tent, no sleeping bag, no dry clothes, no friends (apart from the thousands of new ones disguised as strangers all around us) and only fifty pounds to get me through the weekend. Whilst searching for her, I had kind of presumed that if I'd found her, none of this would matter. Maybe I could stay with her. Maybe she could provide food, shelter, drugs and companionship for the weekend. But the reality was, that I didn't know her at all. We'd had a ten-minute conversation a few weeks before - a quick kiss and that was all. But there I was, and knowing full-well that honesty is the best policy, I hit her with the truth.

It didn't go down well at all.

"But where are you going to sleep?" She said. "Who comes to a festival alone? What on earth are you going to do?" She was actually pretty annoyed. I told her not to worry and that I'd work it out, and that I'd already met a shit-ton of amazing people just trying to find her. I was sure that if I followed my nose something would happen and it would all end well (ever the optimist). Her mood then changed again and seemed to go from being annoyed to actual pity. She said "you can stay with us but you're not staying in my tent. Follow me." She promptly turned on her heels and walked off into the mass of people.

Mary walked through the festival differently. For the last few hours, I'd been stumbling around with no particular destination and with my head darting back and forth trying to take everything in. Bumping into people, I followed the slow ambling pace of the crowd, dodging the massive puddles and muddy vats. Mary, on the other hand, cut through the crowds with a fast, determined pace. It felt like people were actually parting for her. She was moving fast. I did my best to keep up with her, my eyes on her wings. We seemed to walk for a long time, pretty much in silence. With Mary leading the way, it was hard for me to be heard. After a while, I shouted "WHEREABOUTS WE HEADING?" I was mainly trying to keep the mood up. She didn't turn around but said something that sounded like "the Christian field". I didn't pay it much attention as I'd presumed that I'd heard it wrong, or that it was a joke.

It wasn't.

Shortly afterwards, we arrived at a small circle of tents in the corner of a field. In actual fact, it felt like it must have been the corner of the entire festival. It was dark and there was a fire with a handful of people sat around it. There were two big tipi tents and a scattering of smaller tents. This was pre-pop-up so think more triangles than domes. Mary took my bag and put it in her tent (giving me some hope) and then took me to the fire and introduced me to Joseph. He was sat on a tree trunk, giving him a bit of height over the rest of the folk around the fire. She introduced me and my predicament, and he was even less impressed than Mary was. I could tell by the way he was looking at me that he thought I was an idiot. He said "we are Christians and so we will be Christian." (it turned out I had heard correctly) "You can stay with us for the weekend but you can't stay in Mary's tent. We'll find something else for you." He followed it with "who comes to a festival alone?" I was offered some tasty pasta and a seat around the fire. It was warm. I was also starving and it was nice to take a load off. Pretty soon afterwards, Joseph got his Bible out and suggested that we all pray.

I've never been a fan of organised religion. I wasn't raised religiously or baptised in any church. Both my Primary and Secondary School were half-heartedly Christian. We sung hymns and were told the stories from the bible but it wasn't too pushy or, in fact, believable. I'd only ever been to church a few times with school or with Cub Scouts. I basically believed in Jesus in the same way I believed in Santa Claus. I stopped believing in both around the same time as well. That said, I do have my own set of beliefs. One of them is 'each to their own' and I've got absolutely no problem with other people believing whatever the hell they want to believe. Worship away my friends - that's absolutely fine by me. My only problem comes when people try to force their set of beliefs on others. That's not cool. In short, don't try to convince me to worship your God and I won't call bullshit on your charade.

So, there I was, with Mary and Joseph (I know, right?!), eating their food and warming by their fire. They were being hospitable and, in turn, I was being respectful. I sat through two prayers before I could catch Mary's eye and do the universal nod that translated as 'let's get the fuck out of here'. She smiled and stood up. Thank the Lord. I also thanked Joseph for the food and we headed back into the party.

During the walk back in, Mary slowed her pace and we walked side by side. She still wanted to talk about my predicament. I thought that was all sorted, and all I had to do was to sneak past Joseph into Mary's tent, but she was concerned about my lack of funds, clothes and sleeping equipment. She explained that food at festivals was expensive (little did she know what the future would hold for festival food price inflation) and once I'd bought some waterproofs (it was still raining and word was that it wasn't going to be stopping any time soon) and a sleeping bag, I'd barely have enough left for food. Apparently, I couldn't rely on her friends - Christian or not, they were also on a tight budget. "No worries." I told her. In actual fact, I'd already put a plan together when I was walking around looking for her earlier. I'd seen a stall selling cornish pasties and bacon rolls for one pound each. I'd also seen a bar selling bottles of wine for a tenner. I was planning on getting a bottle of wine there and then. Then, for the next three days, I'd have a bacon roll for breakfast, pasty for lunch, pasty for dinner, and a bottle of wine a day. This all added up to a total of forty-nine pounds so I still had a quid left: sorted!

Mary didn't like my plan. She didn't think that Joseph would approve either. Without being rude, I explained that maybe we were both looking for different things from the weekend ahead. If I was going to have a religious experience, I would imagine it was going be off my head on a dance floor. My only minor concern about my so-called predicament was that I didn't have any drugs or money to buy them, but I was confident they would materialise. "Just look around." I said. "We're at Glastonbury." As I scanned the crowds in front of me, the excitement hit me like a drum. I stopped in my tracks and shouted it "WE'RE AT GLASTONBURY!"

In response, a stranger shouted back "YES WE ARE!" And handed me a spliff. I took a drag and went to pass it back but the giver was long gone. I had a few more puffs, offered it to Mary, who wasn't having any of it, then passed it to another stranger. They smiled, gave me a hug and went on their merry way. At that moment, I realised I was exactly where I wanted to be. It wasn't a predicament at all: it was fucking amazing.

As we got further into the festival, it started to get busier, noisier and more exciting. I needed a piss so we stopped at some toilets and Mary said she would wait while I did what I needed to do. We were at a crossroads where four major walkways met and it was hectic. Coming out of the toilets, I examined the crowd but couldn't see Mary anywhere, and I wasn't one hundred percent sure which way we had come from. What I did see, though, was the wine bar. It was pretty hard to miss; it had massive inflatable bottle of wine coming out of the top of it and it was banging out a Beatles tune at top volume. A small crowd of folk had congregated and were drinking wine and dancing. It looked great. There at the crossroads, I felt like I had a decision to make and my actions would determine the outcome of my weekend. I looked again for Mary. I couldn't see her. I went to the wine bar.

I never saw Mary Fairy again.

I'm not actually sure if Mary skipped out on me or I skipped out on her. If it was the latter, I apologise. It was a bit of a dick move. But in all honesty, it needed to be done. It's not the kind of move I'd make these days but I was sixteen, and I had a lot to learn. What happened over the next three days changed me as a person and changed the direction of my life. I'm confident in saying that it made me who I am today or, at the very least, it put me on this course.

My actual memory of the festival is blurred and faded. I know I saw Radiohead ("Can you turn on the light so we can see the people?"). We also saw Beck and countless bands, DJs and performers I'd never heard of before. It was also that weekend that I first appreciated Reggae. Up until that time, I didn't even think I liked Reggae. I do. I fucking love it. It was like I heard it there for the first time. I felt it. I walked, danced, talked, walked, drunk, smoked, walked, talked, kissed (not snogged - see, I was already learning). I slept where I ended up - generally on sofas in the back of cosy late-night tea tents. One night a stranger/friend let me sleep in their car. It wasn't really an issue. I met so many incredible people from all walks of life - they all did such interesting things with their lives. It was truly eye-opening.

My blurry memories of that Glastonbury now blur into other blurry memories of all the Glastonbury festivals since, because I have never missed one. Every now and then they have a fallow year (the festival takes a year off to let the land have a rest) but, to date, over the course of twenty years, I have attended sixteen Glastonburys and counting.

I've written countless songs about Glastonbury and it continues to be a highlight of my year. It's changed a lot over the years. So has the world. So have I. I still have maximum respect for it. It's the greatest party in the world. I'll try and jot down a few of my Glastonbury tales in a nutshell before we crack on with the rest of the book…

The following year I travelled down with Dave Danger. We jumped the fence and invented the free hug. He was hooked, too. For the few years that followed, there was always a stamp blag or a hole in the fence. There was always a way in. Apart from that first ticket from Crystal, I've never bought a Glastonbury ticket. Back in the late '90s it was pretty standard to jump or blag your way in. That's just how it was. That changed in 2002 when the super fence went up alongside a PR campaign telling people you could no longer break in. It was down to the fact that it was getting too popular. Everyone was blagging it and there were too many people. Fair dos. It was then, in 2002, that I started working different jobs in and around the festival in exchange for tickets.

My first job was working for an inflatables company putting up decor around the site. I'd scored the job through a friend and I was on site a week early for the set up. It was that year that I met Banksy. I had a BMX and spent most of the time burning around the site on it. I'm a huge fan of Bansky's work. Back then he wasn't a household name but I knew his work and I knew his identity was very much a secret. I saw a guy putting up a stencil while riding around the site. I recognised the work, realised who it was, and went over for a bit of a chat. Nice guy. I saw him again the following year filling up tents with helium balloons, graffing Banksy on the side, and letting them fly away. He was having trouble holding one of the tents down. I ran over to lend a hand and helped him while he tagged it, and we let it fly away. You know, just helping your favourite artist do his thing. Yes, Glastonbury.

One year, I was working in the Dance Field. I was a late night stage manager doing the overnight shift for the first ever silent Disco in the UK. Nobody knew it was going to go off like it did and somehow I was running the show. I was in charge of ten security guards, fifteen stewards, two hundred pairs of headphones and thousands of baffled ravers. The night went about as smoothly as you'd imagine it would. Apologies to Hexstatic who had a tough time that night.

Around the mid 2000s (more about them in the next chapter), I was managing a band called The Holloways. Their first Glastonbury show was on The Other stage and they smashed it. It was the first time I saw the workings of any of the main stages and full hospitality. As for the backstage bar, don't worry, you're not missing anything. It was nice to set foot on The Other stage, though. I tried to sneak onto the Pyramid but got caught and didn't make it. I'm yet to set foot on that bad boy.

For a three-year spell I worked for a charity called Strummeville. It was set up by the friends and family of Joe Strummer after his departure from Earth. We ran a massive campfire at the back of The Unfairground. I had various roles, from booking bands, collecting firewood, doing sound, making tea, keeping the peace, and keeping the fire burning. I had one job description and that was to make Joe proud. Still one of the best jobs I've ever had. I definitely gave it a good shot.

The first ever Beans on Toast gig was at Glastonbury. It was a spur of the moment thing. I was in a tent called The Banyan Tree Cafe (RIP) and it was open mic. I had a handful of new songs I'd written. I was intending to start a bit of a band and call it Beans on Toast but hadn't put that into action yet. It was a get up and play vibe in the tent. They had a communal guitar that you could borrow so I got up and played the new songs. They went down well. By the end of the first song, I decided that I was going to go it solo. The chap that played after me was an old hippy dude with some brilliantly funny songs. He had enjoyed my stuff and we had a chat about songwriting and what not. He said he only sung about three things: sex, drugs and politics. I pretty much used that as a blueprint for every song I've written since. Thanks, dude - wherever you are.

One of the main things that influenced the new songs I'd written was Billy Bragg's performance in the Leftfield tent the year before. For the first time I saw how music and politics were intertwined and how important it is for us to question those in charge. So, the year after my show in The Banyan Tree, it was a huge honour to be invited to play in the Leftfield tent. It was an actual, proper booking, with my name on the line up and everything. My gig was opening the Leftfield stage on the Thursday and was at some crazy time like 11am. Stupidly, I stayed up all night doing cheap speed and ended up playing a pretty messy and chaotic show. Somehow I was invited back the next year, though, and did a much better job. I've shared the stage with Billy a few times over the years. At times, I have taken part in 'Billy's Round Up' and would go as far to call him a friend. That's not me name dropping. I just want you to know that those dreams are completely tangible and within grasp. I went from standing, watching, and being inspired, to writing, singing and performing for other people. Anyone can be a folk singer. That's a lesson that I learnt.

After the first gig on the Leftfield stage, I've been lucky enough to get booked every year. That includes the year I wrote "Can't get a gig at Glastonbury" (turns out I was just being impatient). I've battled power cuts in Hell, had Brexit breakfasts at Greenpeace, I've gone down the Rabbithole, sung at the Bandstand, I've bimbled around The Bimble Inn, I've watched the Monday morning sunrise from the Stone Circle, and I still love to walk around the festival alone. Who goes to a festival alone? I do. Glastonbury now falls

14

on the same weekend as Lizzy Bee's Birthday. She's the love of my life and we go together. Don't you just love a good coincidence?

Trying to plan the future is an awful way to spend the day but I can only hope that I'll be back at Glastonbury this year, next year, and so on and so forth, to make some more stories and meet more people. I'll meet you there - Thursday, 6pm, The Tiny Tea Tent.

JELLICOE,
NAMBUCCA AND FROG

I'm not intending for this book to be in chronological order. It's just a collection of stand-alone stories, most of which have taken place since I've started going under the moniker of Beans on Toast. However, from that first Glastonbury, to me coming up with the stupid name, a lot went down. As a result, and for the sake of clarity, I'll recap those years in this chapter. They can be broken down into Jellicoe, Nambucca and FROG.

Jellicoe was my first ever band. We were a three-piece grunge band. Me, Jot and Dave. Best mates. We actually decided to be in a band, and tell everyone else we were in a band, before we owned instruments or could play a note. We used to graffiti the band's name around school and we probably thought we were well cool. Musically, I'd already been through various phases in my life. As a young child, I loved the Country music my dad played me and would sing along with Randy Travis at the top of my lungs in Dad's car. In my early teens, I became obsessed with Hip hop - Wu Tang Clan's '36 Chambers' and Snoop Dog's 'Doggy Style' being personal favourites. Hip hop was perfect rebellion music in comparison to the safe Country songs. It was badass and I loved it. Pre-Jellicoe, Dave and I actually wrote a rap (I can still remember it word for word) about how we were pimps and gangstas, with guns and bitches. But, of course, we weren't; we were skinny white virgins in school uniforms. It took us a while to work that bit out, though.

Thinking back now, in 1994, when Kurt Cobain died, I couldn't care less. I had no time for 'guitar' music as I would have called it, then. I'd never even listened to a Nirvana song. But in the following years, that changed. It was Jot's brother, Rich, who first played me Nirvana, The Stone Temple Pilots, Dinosaur Jr and the like. It would have been the same sort of time that adolescence kicked in and I started to think about who I was in the world; I wasn't a gangsta. I did actually like this music, guitars and all. It felt a bit more real and relatable. The more I listened, the more I liked. It was also around this time that two important things happened and they both went hand in hand: I started to smoke pot and I started to listen to The Doors. I was transported by Jim Morrison's words, poetry and general attitude to life. He became my hero. When I smoked my first ever spliff down Rayne Park, I decided that I loved getting stoned. Still do. When it came to us deciding to be a band, straight away I said I wanted to be the singer - not really because I thought I could sing, but because I wanted to write the words. I wanted to come up with that shit. Dave and Jot took drums and bass respectively and Jellicoe was born.

We scraped together funds from our weekend factory jobs and bought some cheap instruments. We then started rehearsing at Lake and Elliot's. I say rehearsing but, to begin with, that's somewhat misleading. We actually wrote five songs before we realised that the bass and guitar have to play the same notes for it to resemble what you'd call music, and not just noise. Once we cracked that, though, we wrote and rehearsed religiously. We got our hands on an old lorry container. It was a crazy bargain from some old dude who'd sound proofed it because he was moving house and needed to get rid of it. He was even willing to deliver it. We stuck it in Jot's back garden and 'The Jam Room' was born.

We all honed our skills and learnt our instruments together so, although none of us were particularly great players, we worked well as a unit. We kept the songs simple and got to the point where we could pretty much make up new songs on the spot. That was it. We'd done it. We were a band. So, we did what bands do, and started playing gigs.

One of Jellicoe's first shows was opening for Planet Empathy at The Army and Navy. Looking back, it probably sounded pretty shocking but I thought it was incredible. I was hooked. We were writing more, the songs were getting better, and it quickly became the only thing I gave a shit about. By this time, the three of us had all started Braintree College and had a large group of friends, many of whom were in bands themselves. Along with bands like Janet Theory, Waster (Jot's brother's band) and Union Kid, we started playing all over Essex. We'd play shows together and go out to watch each other's bands. We had a massive group of mates - 'The Mudhills Crew', as we were called. A rag-tag bunch of grebos and stoners. Good times were had. Due to the lack of venues in Braintree, we'd often hire a coach to transport mates to our gigs, always out of our own pockets. We all had weekend work and would put all the cash into the band. The gigs would always lose money but that was never the point. Jellicoe only played a handful of shows outside of Essex and most of those were in London.

One of those said shows was at The Bull & Gate in Kentish Town, for the Fierce Panda label. It was reviewed by The NME which, at the time, was a very well respected music mag. It said "Braintree's Jellicoe have brought all their mates with them. Oh, it's a fearful sight. This mob of tangled teenagers have had their bottle of White Lightning (each) in the van, been sick behind the kebab shop and are flopping and stumbling all over." Sounds about right.

One fond Jellicoe story is the day that John Peel phoned my house. Dave and I had recently made a trip to London to tell the world who we were. We bunked the train up and spent the day knocking on doors of record labels with our new demo. I think we were both surprised how well it went. Just by being ballsy, and blagging a few receptionists, we managed to get into the buildings of a few major labels and actually hand-delivered the demo to the A&R guys at Food Records and Deceptive Records. With our new-found confidence, we strolled into Radio 1 and asked "Is John Peel here?" Apparently, we'd just missed him but the nice receptionist, Claire, said we could leave music or letters in his pigeon hole. So we did. About a month later, I was at home eating breakfast and I answered the (landline) phone. A strangely familiar voice asks for Jay or Dave. This was obviously quite weird as I lived with my parents at the time, not Dave. He then introduced himself as "John Peel from the amazing Radio 1". I nearly choked on my Weetabix. He'd listened to the CD and wanted to play a track. Bang on. It eventually led to us getting a few plays and a John Peel session a bit further down the line - something I'm still very proud of.

We continued the band right through college and beyond. After college, we went into full-time factory work and started saving up funds to move to London in order to take the band to the next level. Quickly, I fell into the monotonous factory job cycle of spending everything I'd earned every weekend. I was getting shitfaced to keep my sanity. It's a dangerous game, played by many, and with the running costs of the band, saving wasn't going well. In fact, savings were non-existent. One day something snapped. I remember it clearly. Both Dave and I were working in a factory that made office divides. For nine-hour shifts, we'd be stapling and gluing bits of wood together. They'd go on to be covered in material and then shipped off so that they could

19

divide other poor folk who probably hated their jobs, too. It was soul-destroying. But as you do, we had a laugh with it. Dave and I, being in same job together (which was a rare treat), would get stoned, and we'd piss about to help pass the time. On this one day, the boss dude had enough of us laughing and smiling and put us to work in the wood shop, sweeping up. There was a constant supply of woodchip and sawdust coming from the saws – the floor was covered. It made the job pretty much impossible and completely demoralising, hence it being a punishment. We realised that if we did it that day, we'd be doing it forever. I'm not even sure if we said anything to each other - I'd like to think we just knew. We looked at each other, dropped the brooms, and walked out.

I told my folks that I was moving to London even though I didn't have any money. It was something I needed to do and I needed to do it right then. It's worth mentioning, here, that my folks have always been incredibly supportive of everything I've done, especially with music. Dad gave me my first guitar, and both Mum and Dad would drive Jellicoe to gigs, rehearsals, and what-not (Mum actually came up with the name Jellicoe). They still come to as many Beans on Toast gigs as they can. Just a few weeks ago, they hand-made a Beans on Toast T-shirt for my nephew, Sy, and brought him along to Blissfields festival to see me play. They'll read this book for sure. Hi Mum. Hi Dad. Thanks for everything! However, the idea of their nineteen-year-old son upping to the big smoke, without a penny in his pocket, didn't fill them with joy. They were both born and bred Londoners so understood the appeal, but also the dangers of the city. They were working solidly to pay the mortgage and were in no position to lend. Even still, Mum spoke to her brother and Uncle Terry lent me one thousand pounds that I could pay back in instalments when I got my shit together.

Although moving to London ended up being a brilliant life decision, my first trip there didn't go well. Dave and I headed down for the day to check out potential flats. We bought a copy of 'Loot' (now defunct due to the internet - but it was like eBay or Zoopla in printed form) and arranged a few viewings. The first was in West London, near Gloucester Road tube station. Walking up the stairs, into the light, I could see cops everywhere. I didn't really think much about it. It was the big city and I presumed they were on some big, important case, nothing to do with me. I happily went to walk down the road when a sniffer dog ran over, smelt my pocket, and sat down next to me. Oh dear. The cop explained that the dog had detected drugs on me and that gave them the right to search me. I was taken off to a private room. I mentally scanned my pockets and realised that yes, the dog was right. I had a spliff's worth in the little watch pocket of my jeans. It was a teeny-tiny piece of hash. I pretty much expected the cops to laugh, it was London after all. Surely, they had bigger fish to fry than a nineteen-year-old with a pebble in his pocket. I pulled it out, showed it to the copper, and said "this is all I have mate."

He arrested me.

In the car on the way to the nick, I told him that I thought it was a bit much and surely there were a lot more serious crimes going on. He explained to me that I was a statistic. Yes, much worse shit was going down all over the city, but that dog cost a fortune to be at that tube station and they needed arrests to warrant it – they would take every arrest they could. The cop actually apologised. I ended up with a caution (which means very little) and was locked up for five hours. When I did get out, I found Dave waiting outside. It was late and we'd missed all our viewings, so we headed back to Braintree. Not the greatest start but we weren't deterred and went back the next day without any hash in our pockets and we had another bash – this time we were a little more successful and we found a flat in Stamford Hill. To be honest, I think I dodged a bullet. At least I didn't end up living in West London.

Moving to London turned out to be the the death of the band. We gave it a shot but the city's not for everyone. After a blast, Jot moved back to Essex. It was fair enough. Jot's still my best mate and lives happily with his wonderful wife and kids. Before we called it a day, we did play a few more gigs and we recorded and released an album and a few EPs. They're actually up on Spotify and iTunes and what-not. I'd suggest you have a listen but you won't believe it's me because back then I used to sing with a fake American accent. Weird.

Dave and I fell in love with the city. We moved through various cheap houses and various random jobs in markets, shops, pubs and clubs. I really found my calling when I got a job handing out flyers for an indie club. It was the best job I'd ever had. You were outside, could drink on the job and basically had to talk to people. During the week, I'd flyer outside gigs. I soon realised that if I asked everyone going in if they had a spare ticket for a music-loving flyer-guy, I could get into the show for free. I saw Bob Dylan, The Flaming Lips, Everclear and countless other bands that way. At weekends, I'd flyer for clubs either in Camden or The West End, approaching folk and convincing them to go into the club for a party. I was young, excitable, single, and horny as fuck. I basically spent my time chatting up girls. After the flyer shift finished, I'd get free entry and a few free drinks at the club. Once I'd arrived, half the folk in there were the ones I'd convinced to go. It made for some great nights. My success as a flyer-guy meant I got bumped up to email-collector. The internet was still a new thing. This was pre-social media but everyone had a Hotmail address, and every decent club wanted them for their mailing lists. So, I'd walk around the club collecting email addresses (chatting up girls) - another very enjoyable job. Then I was bumped up again and I started organising the flyering. Then, I started running the actual club nights. It was a lot of fun and all pretty easy to understand. I left the company I was working for and Dave and I started our own club night.

Our first night was called sTatiK (check out the incorrect spelling and crazy use of capitals!). It was at The Garage in Highbury. We hung white bed sheets over the walls, threw up some random projections and played a mixed bag of fun tunes to the Friday night crowd. It worked. It was fun and the money was decent, mainly because Dave and I did everything ourselves: we flyered all week at gigs and clubs, we ran the night, and we DJed it. This was 2003, a brilliant time for live music and indie nights. The clubs were packed in London at the time. If you were so inclined (and we quite often were) you could go to a club night every night of the week. Mondays at Trash, Tuesdays at Feet First, Wednesdays at Candybox and so on and so forth. Our presence at these nights actually made our own night busier and more well known. Somehow, we'd invented a job that involved going to clubs, getting hammered, and making new friends. We worked as hard as we could at it.

One Sunday afternoon, me, Dave, and a group of mates, strolled into a pub around the corner from our house. We lived in Archway at the time and the pub was on Holloway Road. It was called Nambucca. The place was fucking massive. It was a beautiful, classic boozer with a nice long bar, and a raised level with a tiny stage at the back. A brilliant space. And it was empty, really empty. We spent the afternoon drinking in there and not one other person came through the doors all day. This seemed crazy to us. The manager, and sole member of staff, was a good guy. He explained that he'd just taken the place on and was looking to get it off the ground. Dave and I said we'd throw a party the following Sunday in exchange for free booze all day. He agreed and 'Sensible Sundays' was born.

The following week we took along a guitar and some decks, and we cobbled together a PA from an old stereo and a bass amp. We also invited all our mates. The pub took more money that Sunday than it had in the month and a half since the manager had taken it on. We were given permission to do whatever we wanted. 'Sensible Sundays' became a weekly event and would generally be the last part of a big Saturday night. Each week, we'd take the party to the pub and each week it got busier. Things snowballed. We started to put on more frequent events on weeknights. Then we found out that there were ten rooms upstairs, eight of which were empty. Dave and I moved in and the snowball turned into an avalanche. The manager left (the place was turning into a circus apparently) and our mate Stix took the job which meant we had full control. We'd somehow blagged our own pub.

I lived above that pub for the next five years of my life. They were brilliant, debauched days of sex, drugs and rock'n'roll. Trying to put those years into a paragraph won't do them justice and, to be honest, my memory doesn't serve me particularly well from that period. But, that said, I do know that all the rooms were constantly full of a wonderful mix of characters. Music was written, friends were made, and parties were had. We went from the old stereo, to a legit PA system, we built a new stage, and put on gigs for the likes of Laura Marling, The Maccabees, Florence and The Machine and, of course, Frank Turner. Frank didn't technically have a room at Nambucca, but he might as well have.

I've worked in many boozers since and it still blows my mind to think about the stuff we got away with: it was lawless. Sometimes it would be open all night. Then it would close for a week. The party would move easily between the pub, to the rooms upstairs, and then back down again come morning time. During the Summer, we'd put paddling pools out on the roof. We once threw a sofa out of the top floor window. I have no idea why but I remember the sight of the thing going down. We had an office on the top floor where we ran our operations. As much as we were getting shitfaced a lot, we also had our shit together. Various projects were run from that office, be it band-management, club nights, tours and whatever else. There was always lots going down.

Dave had started drumming in a band called The Holloways and they based themselves out of the pub. I took on the role as manager. We had massive success with a wonderful track called 'Generator' (written at a party in Nambucca, as it goes). Radio stations picked it up, the track went top ten, and the band toured the world. I'm not going to lie, I probably wasn't the best manager, but we did alright.

It was soon after we moved into Nambucca that we started FROG. After the success of our night at The Garage we were on the lookout for a new space. The Mean Fiddler was a one thousand capacity space underneath London's legendary Astoria venue. It was way out of our league, especially when pitching for a Saturday night, which is what we did. Somebody within the company took a shine to us, though, and we got it. A weekly, thousand-cap club night in the West End of London. Shit was getting real.

We had some ideas about what we wanted to do for the night but it really fell into place when I bumped into an old friend from school. I'd blagged my way into an NME awards after-party. Like I said earlier, it was a well-respected music mag back then. These awards were a lot of fun and the booze was free. I was bumbling around chatting up some ladies when Imran came up to me. Imran and I went to the same school but he was a year older. I knew his brother better than I knew him, but it wasn't very often you'd see school mates in London, especially at some NME do. "What the fuck are you doing here?" I said to him.

"I work for the NME." He replied "What are you doing?"

"Drinking your free booze by the looks of it." I said.

It turned out that Imran had recently been taken on as new bands editor of the magazine. He was fresh out of University and a bit of a music industry hot-shot (he went on to do wonderful things). I told him about the pub and club nights, and we arranged to meet up. To cut a long story short, Imran agreed to book the bands for our new club night and come in on the deal. If the new bands editor of the NME asks you to play their club night, you say yes. And everyone said yes.

We kept the formula simple. One band each week went on at 1am and there were DJs either side. We called it FROG because frogs look cool, and that was that. The list of bands is too big to get stuck into but it was the likes of Bloc Party, Babyshambles, The Horrors, The Cribs, Calvin Harris, The Klaxons and Larrikin Love - you get the idea. We were rammed every week. The strange thing about running a club night is that as long as you organise it well beforehand, on the night, you don't really have to do much. I'd just walk around the club getting pissed and high-fiving people. I developed quite the cocaine habit, as well. The safest place in the club to do a line was in our backstage room so anyone who wanted to do a line would generally ask me if I wanted one, too. That way they could get into the room and I was happy to oblige. FROG ran successfully for three years. We called it a day when the smoking ban came into play and Larrikin Love split up. I could feel it in the air; it was time to move on.

It was also during these years that Beans on Toast was - not sure how to word this - born? Created? Invented? It all sounds a bit dramatic but that's where it started. I'd never really stopped writing songs since the Jellicoe days, but the songs I started to write, once I'd moved into the pub, were different. They were more direct and to the point. More English. As mentioned in the previous chapter, I took the songs to Glastonbury and came back with a new found confidence for playing them solo. I started to play at the pub regularly. Bands didn't show up so I'd play. Big bands wanted to play and would fill the place out, I'd support. 3am, I'd play. For the first year, I rarely played anywhere else. I didn't really see the need to. There's an alternate universe somewhere where I'm still living at Nambucca, playing downstairs every other day, and I'd be happy with that. That's not how it went down, though. Instead, Frank Turner asked me to go on tour.

As mentioned, Frank was a regular at the pub. He started coming down to play at 'Sensible Sundays'. At the time, he was in his hardcore/metal band, 'Million Dead'. On the side he'd come to the pub and play solo with his acoustic, doing Neil Young and Counting Crows covers. We became friends. He started to play his own new songs during his acoustic sets, or at the after parties. They were amazing. I loved them. Everybody loved them. They were immediate anthems. As his band split up, everyone at Nambucca encouraged him do his solo thing. To us, that's what he did, we didn't really know much about the band. He disappeared around the country on trains, playing his songs. When he came back, he did a sell out, jam-packed Nambucca gig. Everybody was singing these new-found anthems back at him. It was fucking exciting and I was the support act. Frank's ticket sales quickly outgrew Nambucca but he didn't once forget about me, or any of the others from back in the day. Many friends from the pub have worked, or still work, on Frank's crew. Since then, I've toured with Frank many times around the UK. I've opened for him at Wembley, The O2 and many other arenas. It's safe to say that without Frank putting me in front of so many people, and championing my music back then, my journey would have been a different one. I doubt very much I'd be in the position to feel that people would give a shit if I wrote a book. What a trip! Frank and I are still close friends and have many a musical adventure planned for the future. Even as I write this, there are plans for a 'Sensible Sundays' reunion at The Roundhouse in Camden. The fucking Roundhouse! Who would have thought it?

So, yeah, Nambucca was magical and those days were very special indeed. All but one of the songs from my debut album were written in that building (and there's a lot of tracks on that album). Undoubtedly, it's not the last time you'll hear about the place. Stick me with and I'll tell you about the day the Nambucca burned down.

MDMA

I met a pretty girl at a festival with a bag of MDMA… Chances are, if you're reading this book, you already know that story because I turned that story into a song, and it's probably the most popular song I've ever written. It sounds like all my other songs but, for whatever reason, more people like that one - something resonates. This is great for me as it means I get to travel around, singing that song (and many others) to all sorts of different people in all sorts of different places.

The song itself is a true story, well nearly. It all happened word for word until the last verse. Unfortunately, said girl wasn't mad interested in the morning and she didn't come find me under the tree with a cup of tea. I do like my songs to have happy endings, though, so I fantasised a bit. Maybe it was the last happy ending bit that did the trick - I don't know. I've actually got a couple of songs about that song and a shit loads of stories about it. Two of which I'll share with you in this chapter.

One of the many places that touring with this song took me was to Bedford, cleverly situated in the heart of Bedfordshire. Over the years of travelling with my music, I've learnt not to refer to towns as shitholes, but that's what I would have called it at the time.

It was a rainy Tuesday night in Bedford and we (myself and Bobby Banjo) we're playing downstairs at a venue called Esquires.

It was a bit like a pub or a working men's club. I never saw the actual venue upstairs; we were just playing the bar room - no stage, just a vocal PA kind of gig. It was 5pm when a young kid came into the venue. It was a bit early to expect folks to be coming in for the show. He was maybe sixteen or seventeen and he was hammered. Really hammered – gurning and eyes rolling into the back of his head kind of hammered. So, just to reiterate: 5pm, Bedford, raining, Tuesday, hammered, and he came straight up to me and said "I really love your music man." Now, this is a wonderful thing to hear. Every now and again, people say it to me and it gives me a warm feeling inside. Then, he followed it up with "your music inspired me to start taking drugs."

Not such a wonderful thing to hear.

Now, I love drugs. I'll be straight and tell you that my days of coke, pills and other chemical pleasures are now behind me. That was a personal decision as I'd kind of had my fill, but I still see their place in society and in life in general. I have had a wonderful time on drugs. Some of my greatest thoughts, feelings, and experiences were had while I was high. I understand they are dangerous, that they are addictive, and that they need to be treated with respect. I also understand they are not for everyone. However, I know that at the right time, with the right people, the right drug can be a brilliant and beautiful thing (as in the song). My problem with drugs is that people don't talk about them. People tend to make stupid generalisations. The whole "say no to drugs" thing that they pushed on us at school was as ignorant as the laws that are put in place, and then widely ignored. In short, I'm bang up for open-minded education, letting people experiment with their drugs of choice, and not treating people like idiots.

But, on that rainy Tuesday in Bedford, stood in front of the gurning kid, all of those ideas came crashing down around me. What the fuck was I doing with my life? Why was I travelling around singing songs about how much fun it is to take MDMA? There was the result, right there in front of me.

I wasn't sure what to do. So, I did what any rational, guilt-ridden, grown-up would do. I stayed up all night doing pills with the kids of Bedford.

Only joking. I did the only thing I could do. After getting the kid a glass of water and giving him a quick chat about the wonders and dangers of drug use, I wrote a song. It's called "The Children of Bedford" and it was my first ever anti-drugs song. I wrote it in an attempt to clear up any mixed messages that I might have previously sent out.

I'd generally play the two songs back to back. Sometimes I'd actually play one song in the middle of another. I call it a song sandwich. Quite often on stage, I'll tell this story as well, just to give the song a bit of an introduction. Inevitably, the song and/or story got back to the children of Bedford who were at the show. I've spoken to a few of them over the years when our paths have crossed. This all happened many moons ago, but just a few months ago I got an email from a girl at Warwick University. It turns out that she is now the girlfriend of someone from that gig. She runs a podcast and wondered if I'd want to chat to her about it. She said:

My boyfriend is a huge fan of yours and, as it happens, it was him and his friends who were the inspiration for your song "The Children of Bedford". My boyfriend just graduated from Warwick with a First in Film and Literature, achieving the highest grade in his year. His friend (the kid who approached you) has just graduated with a First in English Literature from the University of Bristol. I was wondering how it makes you feel that the children (as they were at the time when they were wasted on ecstasy at your gig) of Bedford have been incredibly successful in their lives. Perhaps you'd be willing to talk to me a little about the writing of the song.

What a great email to get. I, of course, stopped by for a chat and, as I said to her, at no point did I think that they were on course for some kind of life disaster. I'd like to think that if that were the case, I would have done something more substantial than fetch a glass of water and write a song. I also said that I wasn't at all surprised that people who liked to get a bit wasted at gigs in their teens went on to do wonderful, academic things. I could use a First in English Literature. It might make this book a bit more remarkable. That's for sure.

~

"I need to talk to you."

She didn't want to talk to me, she *needed* to talk to me. I could tell. She'd said it in a very definite way. This was in Manchester at The Night & Day. I'd just come off stage and this girl had come straight up to me. It felt serious. I suggested we go outside where it would be a bit quieter. Once we were out there, she told me a story...

She'd met a boy at a festival and she had a bag of MDMA. They'd started to get it on and were kind of living out the song. A few people along the way have told me how similar my song is to their own stories. Again, it's a great thing to hear and gives me that same warm feeling inside. However, at this point, the girl had never heard the song. She was into this boy and decided to go back to his tent with him. Once there, the boy got his guitar out and sung the song "I met a pretty girl at a festival..." Then, he told the girl that he'd written the song about her. Okay. Quite a smooth move, I thought. This guy was thinking on his feet. And it worked. She loved it. She loved it enough to get it on with the boy that night in the tent. She also liked it enough to stay in touch and, before they knew it, they were in a full-blown, loving relationship. Great news. Now, in my opinion, this would be a great time to come clean about the song – 'fess up, laugh it off and carry on. No problem. But no, that's not what he did. Instead, he took another one of my songs, a song called "My New Number One". It was the first song I ever wrote about Lizzy Bee, and he changed Lizzy's name to her name. He then claimed he'd written her another song.

Not cool. Not cool at all.

All of a sudden, this guy wasn't a smooth dude thinking on his feet. He was just an unoriginal, lying douchebag. But the girl had no idea. She loved it. She had two songs written about her by her wonderful new boyfriend. She was so happy about it, in fact, that she told one of her friends about it and started to sing her the song. It was at this point that her friend broke the news. She had heard these songs before… maybe this guy hadn't written these songs. Her friend suggested she get on YouTube and have a little listen to Beans on Toast. Which she did. She found out the truth about the boy and the truth about the songs, and she also found out that I was playing in Manchester, where she lived, that very night! In fact, it was just down the road. So, she called the guy, ended the relationship and headed down to my gig. She walked straight up to me and said:

"I need to talk to you."

Wow. Alright. What to do now, I thought. I was in a loving relationship so it's not like I could pick up where the boy left off and start writing her new songs. I'm pretty sure that's not what she was expecting anyway. When I asked her what she wanted to do about this weird situation that we found ourselves in, she wasn't really sure either. She said she just felt that she should come and explain it to me, especially since I was playing down the road on the day she found out the truth.

I suggested that we call the guy up, see what he had to say for himself, and she thought that was a great idea. Limp-dick prick that he was, he didn't answer the phone. Which is a shame but I left a great voicemail about originality, honesty and the simplicity of the chords G, C and D. If he could play them, he could make up his own song about his girl, and then he wouldn't be in the shit house.

All this went down a long time ago and pretty much immediately I started to tell the story at gigs. I'd tell it in the little breakdown before the last verse. You might have even heard it before. This part was usually the end of the story and I'd finish on the bit about the phone call, get a few laughs (hopefully), and then drop into the last verse, wrapping up the song.

A few years later, I was back in Manchester and playing a venue called The Ruby Lounge. I decided it'd be a good time to tell what I'd named in my head "The Manchester story". When I got to the end, and the bit about the phone call, a voice came from the back of the room and shouted "IT WAS ME!"

Luckily, it was a female voice so I decided it must have been the girl who'd told me the story rather than the dude I'd just called a limp-dick prick in front of three hundred people. The girl came forward and I invited her up on stage. Firstly, I asked her to corroborate the story. I'd been telling it for so long I myself wasn't even sure if it had actually happened – having said that, don't let that put you off the rest off the book. I'm pretty sure it's all true. She confirmed that, yes, that was how it went down. I'm pretty sure I asked her about the fate of the boy. I can't remember the outcome, though, as I suddenly realised that the girl was wearing a Beans on Toast T-shirt, and then it dawned on me that she'd bought a ticket and had come to the show as well. So, what had actually happened was that by ripping me off, this guy had actually introduced someone new to my music, and that person bought T-shirts and tickets. This was big news, I pointed this out to the crowd. Then I announced that from then on, anybody, anywhere, was allowed to use any of my songs to get laid; they could go right ahead. Change the names or the places if they needed to, I told them. Do whatever you have to do, and if I sell a T-shirt at the end of it, then everyone's a winner, baby.

~

Typing up that story made me think about how I used that song in a very similar way. Of course, it is my song so I'm allowed. But it's similar all the same.

I'd just written it but was yet to play it to anybody. This was years ago – 2007, maybe? I was playing a brilliant festival called Secret Garden Party. My show was scheduled for Sunday afternoon. On Saturday night, I met a pretty girl with a bag of MDMA. She was ace and once we got chatting and dabbing, we hung out and pulled an all-nighter. I was just going to go straight through until my show that afternoon. Back in those days, I'd play my best shows if I'd been up and on it all night. On a cocktail of drugs, a shit-ton of booze, and two full days of partying without sleep, I'd happily get up and put on an entertaining performance. Some of my favourite shows went down that way, especially at SGP where most of the crowd had been up all night as well. I'd be on the same level. Anyway, that was the plan.

As I said, I had my new song and over the course of the night, I realised how similar the song was to the events of my own night. At one point I nearly told her about the song, but I stopped myself, figuring it would be a nice surprise.

That afternoon, by the time I jumped up on stage, I hadn't left the girl's side all night. We'd been hanging out non-stop since we met. So, when I dedicated my first tune to her, and sung a song about what seemed to be the last twenty-four hours, she was impressed. In her eyes, I must have been making that shit up on the spot, which was crazy because it sounded like a really well-rehearsed, thought-out song. Shit, I thought at the time, this could even go on to be one of the most popular songs I have. I did come clean later that night, though. We laughed it off and carried on. No problem. I don't want to kiss and tell but the night ended well...

I write songs for many reasons. Despite the jokes, I don't do it to sell T-shirts and I don't do it to promote the use of drugs. But, if off the back of my songs people are having good fun and consensual sex, then I'm all for it. That's especially true if one of those people is me.

THE KATE NASH CAR CRASH

"I AM ALIVE."

That was my opening line when I walked on stage at The Hammersmith Apollo. It was the first time I'd ever played a venue of that size or calibre. I was opening for the amazing Kate Nash and I walked on stage soaking wet from head to toe and shouted it at the top of my voice.

Not the usual start to a show, but I'd not had a usual day. In fact, I'd had a brush with death - a high speed brush on the M3.

I'd met Kate a year or so before. We did a few London pub shows together at venues like The Lock Tavern and The Old Queens Head. She was lovely and you could kind of tell it was about to kick off for her. Great songs and a wonderful charm. She must have liked my songs because she asked me to join her on a UK tour. This was just before her debut album, 'Made of Bricks', came out. There was a great excitement around her music but she'd yet to bust open the charts and become a fully fledged pop star and household name. This tour was playing to sold out rooms of around three hundred people. I was opening and Peggy Sue and The Pirates were main support. The tour was a whole load of fun, heading up to Aberdeen and back. At the time, I didn't drive, or own a vehicle, so I called on an old mate from school. Stretch was working in Braintree as a plasterer at the time and had the classic white transit van. The summer before, he began to clear his van out on weekends, stick a mattress in the back, and we did festivals together (more on that later). He was the obvious choice so I asked if he fancied a two week jaunt around the country. He was up for it. We also picked up another schoolmate, Stockley, who had some time off work and was up for splitting the driving. This did mean that one of us had to travel in the back of the van, in the dark, bouncing around on a mattress - but that's how it went. As I said, it was a great tour. I became closer friends with Kate and her band and crew. Soon after the tour, Kate's album came out, followed by the single, 'Foundations', and things blew up. I was very happy for her. She deserved it.

As these things usually go, I didn't see Kate for a while after that. She went off to tour the world. In fact, the next time I saw her was in New York.

I was in New York by accident. I was supposed to be in Barbados. This was towards the end of the FROG days. I'd started pimping myself out for DJ shifts as FROG DJs. Generally, I'd book in a gig then just one or two of us would head down, hang an old FROG banner, and play a bunch of indie tunes from a laptop. It was easy money. It was especially easy on New Year's Eve when everything goes double bubble in the party world. I got a DJ gig at Brixton Academy. Xfm (a popular London indie radio station of the time) were throwing a big party with a bunch of live bands and DJs in the main room. They wanted FROG to host the second room. We blagged a one thousand five-hundred pound fee off them and just Dave and I headed down. We blu-tacked a banner to the wall, stuck The Kooks album on, and spent the night in the main room watching the bands. Then we got paid cash at the end of the night. As I said, easy money. I got home hammered on New Year's Day. Feeling suddenly rich, I decided that I needed a holiday. I'd never been on holiday alone before but I thought that was the sort of character building, interesting adventure that I should have under my belt. So, that evening, while still plastered, I booked myself a solo trip to Barbados, not even sure why I chose there. The flights were expensive but a drunk me found a really cheap hotel. I found all this out the following morning when I woke up hungover and realised my flight left in a matter of hours.

The next time I woke up, I was in JFK airport and getting off a plane for a transfer - it was all a bit of a whirlwind blur. It was 8 o'clock and my next flight left at 8:30. As I cleared US customs, and ran frantically to try and catch the next plane, it didn't feel like I'd planned it very well at all. I presumed I'd missed it when I couldn't find any information relating to the flight. But after some confusion, I found out that I hadn't missed it at all. It was, in fact, at 8:30am the following day. I had twelve hours to spare. I was in New York. Sweet deals.

What do you do with one night in 'The Big Apple'? Well, you definitely don't hang around an airport. So, I jumped in a cab and headed towards Manhattan. I'd been to New York a couple of times before but only for short visits. I knew nothing about the beast of a city that it is. I did, however, know a girl called Chelsea who lived there. I didn't know her that well but I knew she was hot. I actually had a bit of thing for her. What the hell? I gave her a bell.

"I'm in NYC for twelve hours. What shall I do?" I said. She said I should go to the party that her and her mates were all going to. Yes, New York! She sent me a text saying it was at a club called Beatrice. I hailed a taxi (very New York) and headed to meet her.

I don't remember a huge amount about the club. I was told later that I was hanging out with Heath Ledger. Apparently, I kept blagging cigarettes off him and winding him up about something or other. Everyone was pussyfooting around him because he was a big Hollywood celebrity, but I had no idea who he was so he got the same treatment as everyone else (please note that I am nice to strangers). Not sure if it was that, that earnt me some New York cred but I definitely made some new friends as the party went through until the morning. As I departed to catch my flight, Chelsea said that if I ever wanted to go back to NYC for more than twelve hours, I'd be welcome to stay with her. I didn't really want to leave - but hey ho. There we go.

I can be extremely ignorant at times. This is especially true with things like geography. I knew nothing about Barbados; it just sounded like a holiday destination. I knew it was an island but in my head I think I thought it was a tiny little island with nothing but sun, beaches and good times. It turns out there's a lot more to it than that. I still know pretty much nothing about the place. With that in mind, I don't want to talk trash about it or its culture. I just don't know it well enough. But, for me, that trip was a total disaster.

I hadn't changed up any money to the local currency so I hit up an ATM on arrival at the airport. My card was blocked due to bizarre patterns of use and it wouldn't give me any cash. One long, boring phone call to my bank later, and I was informed that it would take twenty-four hours to reset my card. Nightmare.

I had twenty pounds in my wallet so I changed that up and headed to the taxi rank. I told the taxi driver the address of my hotel and he wouldn't believe me. He really didn't want to take me to that part of the island. I presumed this was only because I didn't have enough cash so I started laying on the charm. He was a funny chap and we were having a bit of a joke about it but I soon realised that he was strongly suggesting that I didn't go to that area. "Not safe," he said.

I told him not to worry, that I was from Essex. "I got this" I said. At some point, he looked down, he took one look at my shorts, freaked out, opened the back door of his cab and hustled me in. He chucked my bag in the boot, jumped in the driver seat, and took off out of the airport at high speed. He looked worried. Even though he seemed like a kind and caring man, I was sure I was being kidnapped.

He pulled over just outside of the airport, turned to me and said "we need to get you some new shorts." What kind of kidnapping was this? As per usual, I was wearing a pair of cut off army shorts. I've been wearing this style of shorts since I was sixteen. I find them comfortable and convenient (naturally, I've got a pair on as a write this). He then went on to explain that in Barbados army camouflage is used as gang colours. He also explained it was a big deal. It had actually become illegal to wear it. My shorts had basically put me in the firing line of local gangs and the police alike. Shit me. I was definitely not in Essex anymore. The problem was, of course, that I didn't have any money or any access to any money. I was traveling light and didn't have any other shorts to change into. I showed the guy exactly how much money I had and told him again where I needed to go. No way in the world was he taking me to that address in those shorts. He drove off, parked outside a shop, and made me stay in the car while he went inside. He came out with a pair of bright yellow swimming shorts and threw them in the back. What a legend! Once in my new, safe swimmers, I wondered if I could start my holiday. Where were the beaches and the good times at?

The other direction apparently. Where I was staying was a four-hour drive away from where most of the tourists would holiday. A four-hour drive? What the fuck? I thought it was a little island. I was surprised they even had so many cars, let alone motorways and gang colours. There wasn't really much I could do, though. I knew the guy was driving me for a lot less than the actual fare, so off we went. It was a long, hot drive to my destination and the hotel turned out to be a bit of a dive. I've stayed in plenty of cheap hotels before and since, though, so that wasn't a big problem. I bid the kind taxi driver farewell and checked in.

It's with a heart full of regret that I inform you that I used to have dreadlocks - scraggy, natty, dirty dreads grown using the simple art of not touching my otherwise thin straight and wiry hair. Looking back, it was probably a mistake, but whatever. We live and learn. But at this point in my life, alone on my solo, character-building holiday, I had dreads, no money and an afternoon in paradise (?). The lady at the hotel told me how to get to the nearest beach. It was a long walk, and I was advised that it wasn't the best beach on the island, but I headed out anyway. I'm not sure if it was the white guy with dreads, or the silly shorts, or the Englishman in me, but I stood out like a sore thumb.

"Yo, Dread Man" someone shouted. I hadn't made it to the end of the road when they came running up and followed it with "you wanna buy some weed?" I didn't have any money and the idea of being stoned at that moment was not appealing at all. I told the guy I was fine but he was strolling next to me telling me how good his weed was. Apparently, it was really good. He didn't believe me when I said I didn't have any money.

Instead, he said "you want some coke?"

Apparently, his coke was also good - the best, in fact. The guy wasn't threatening at all, quite the opposite actually. He was all smiles and I believed that his weed and coke were top quality. I stopped walking and said one hundred percent no. I was not interested. I thought this would put an end to the exchange but it was like the guy couldn't hear me. Every twenty seconds, he'd start again. "Want some weed?" He just kept going, so I started walking again and he was off with me, right by my side "want some coke?"

Then, all of a sudden, someone else shouted from the distance "Yo Dread Man, you want some weed?" Almost as if he couldn't see the other guy. He came bounding over and walked to my other side. Apparently, his weed was the best and, who would have thought it, he had coke as well. The whole thing got crazy repetitive and monotonous. By the time I'd got to the beach, I had five guys surrounding me offering weed and coke. Again, I didn't feel particularly threatened, but it was far from ideal and I didn't really know how to diffuse the situation.

I got to the beach, left my t-shirt and trainers on the sand and went in for a swim. That seemed like a great plan. My new buddies didn't really react much. They just waited patiently with my shoes and t-shirt as I walked off into the sea. It had been a pretty hectic forty-five minute walk but, as I'm sure you know, the sea has a wonderful all-encompassing effect. It was a hot day and the sea was clear and empty, so I walked out and started to swim. It was great: peaceful and calming. I figured it'd be cool, I'd just sit it out for one night and find an ATM the next day. Maybe I could look at getting to the other side of the island. Maybe I would buy some weed but, for now, I'd just swim and prepare myself for the hectic walk back to the hotel. I was lying on my back pondering these thoughts when I heard the massive roar of an engine. It appeared out of nowhere and came flying towards me. I span around to see a jet ski coming full pelt in my direction. Before I really had time to think, the jet ski had reached me, slowed down and stopped right in front of me. I looked up at the chap riding it. He, in turn, looked back at me. Then he said "wanna buy some weed, Dread Man?"

I needed to get my haircut.

I stayed in Barbados for a week. A couple of times I got the long taxi drive to the other side of the island. The hotels that side were way too expensive and it didn't take me long to realise it wasn't really my vibe over there anyway. I spent most of my days dodging the dealers on the way to shop and then reading on my hotel's tiny balcony. It wasn't all bad but it wasn't great either. It certainly wasn't my dream holiday. I needed to change it up. I kept thinking about Chelsea and my wild night out in New York. I looked into it and my flight home was also stopping in New York. If I could find a cheap flight to New York, I could spend my second week there and then still catch my flight home. Sweet. I was out of there.

I put the plan into place and headed back to 'The Big Apple'. Once I booked the flights, I had a little look to see what was going down while I was there. It turns out that Kate Nash was playing at The Bowery Ballroom on the evening that I arrived. I legged it over from the airport. Unfortunately, I missed the show but snuck into the venue while people were still milling around. As I mentioned, I'd become friends with Kate, her band and crew. Everyone was doing the pack down so I jumped on in.

"What the fuck are you doing here, Beans??!!"

I told them about my misadventures in Barbados and how I might have missed the show but still had a week in NYC. They had an after party planned so I headed there with them. That was Kate's first big visit out to the States and she was also going to be in NYC for a week doing press and being wined and dined by the label. I ended up hanging out all week in fancy bars and restaurants drinking and eating for free with that gang. Chelsea joined us and it felt like I'd spun my holiday around into a success. One night, in a classic American pizza restaurant, I was chatting with Kate about how they'd just announced a huge UK tour with Hammersmith Apollo as the London date. I was actually joking when I asked to open the show. I presumed by that point there would be labels, management and promoters who didn't want a swearing, drunk punk on the bill of a sold-out mainstream pop concert. But Kate thought it'd be a good idea (she was a little drunk at the time) and agreed.

Fast forward a few months. The holiday was firmly in the rear-view mirror and I was back at home in Holloway. The Hammersmith show was just over a week away. I was excited and looking forward to it. It was sold out and was going be the biggest gig in the most prestigious venue that I'd played. Then I got a phone call from Kate.

"Where are you?"

I could tell I'd fucked up. "I'm at home," I said. "The gig's not until next week, isn't it?"

"Yeah but you're opening on the whole tour. You're supposed to be playing tonight in Glasgow."

Fuck. It was 4pm. I was supposed to be on stage at 6:45pm. No way in the world was I going make it. I was happy (I'd got the whole tour), confused (how didn't I know that?), and annoyed (I'd missed the show and let people down.) I apologised profusely and explained that I thought I was just doing London. Kate was cool about it. It was too late to do anything that night but she wanted to know if I wanted to join the tour the following day in Newcastle. Fuck yeah, I did. No one could have stopped me.

I still didn't own a vehicle or know how to drive. I needed to put a plan together fast. The first person I spoke to was Ally Wolf - an absolute legend and a dear friend of mine. He was a Nambucca resident and managed a band called SixNationState. They had a band van and I thought maybe we'd be able to use it. The van was out of action but Ally said he was free. If I could find some wheels, he'd be up for driving. Next up I called maths-genius, life-winner and all round superhero, Johnny Manning of the band Captain Black (also a dear friend to this day. If this book ever gets a launch party it will be held at the brand new bookshop that he and his wife have just opened). They had a van, yes we could borrow it - no problem. The van was a bit knackered but had heart and was reliable enough for a trek up and down the country. Ally was added to the insurance and we were all set. First thing the next morning, we hit the road.

The tour was brilliant. The crowds were quite young, but the audiences were bigger than those I'd played to before, and the shows went down a treat. I got a feel for the big rooms which made me even more excited about the upcoming Apollo show. As tours do, the whole thing flew by in a blur. The night before the London date we were in Portsmouth at the Guild Hall. I sung a new song that I'd written called "Health and Safety". It's an upbeat, cheery number about paedophiles, terrorists and disease set around a car crash on the M4. I made a joke that we would be driving on the M4 the following day before I played it. Terrible joke. Especially since, as Ally pointed out, we'd actually be driving back up the M3. I told you I'm terrible at geography.

On the day of the big show, it was raining. We woke up in a Travelodge just outside of Pompey and hit the road. The tour had been a blast. The van had done us proud and we were on our way to play my biggest show to date. Ally was driving. I was DJing. Life was great. And then, screeeeeech, "What the fuck?" We were skidding. We were in the middle lane of the motorway and we skidded into the fast lane. We were surrounded by cars all doing seventy. Amazingly, they managed to dodge around us. Ally spun the wheel. We careered back into the middle of the road. The steering went and the wheel was doing nothing.

"I've lost control!" Ally said and the van went into a full on spin. Ally and I looked at each other then instinctively leant in and tightly hugged. It all happened very fast. My life didn't flash before my eyes but I was scared shitless and kind of accepted that I was probably going to die. I actually thought about the gig. Maybe I'm not going get to play Hammersmith Apollo. BANG! We hit something. Our grip on each other became even tighter as insanely loud scraping noises filled the whole van. Then all of a sudden...the noises stopped. The van stopped. It felt like the whole world stopped. It was a stillness like I'd never experienced before or since. We were just two grown men holding each other in a van while Belle and Sebastian played gently in the background.

The world slowly started spinning again and still locked in our embrace, Ally said "are you alright?"

Yes. somehow I was. "Are you?"

Yep, it seemed Ally was as well. We slowly let go of each other but something wasn't right. The van seemed to be higher than it should be. It was at a funny angle and the floor was all fucked up. Slowly, we got out the van. It was clear that no other cars were involved. Thank fuck. Somehow we'd survived. Not sure if I've mentioned that I'm an idiot, but I didn't even have my fucking seat belt on. It seems that we'd hit a skid on the motorway. As we were taking a corner, we'd spun around the road and come off then hit the crash barrier. We'd hit the barrier at the start and the van had pretty much done a rail slide (Tony Hawk style) for a few meters along the barrier before coming to a stop. We were alive. Nobody was hurt. The van was fucked. It started to rain.

We called the police. I managed to process the information and the world started to regain its regular speed until it was back to its usual pace. I quickly realised how lucky we both were. A motorway patrol car arrived. The chap didn't really say much considering how mental the situation was. I wasn't sure how people were supposed to react but I guess he saw that stuff (and much worse) everyday. He said that since nobody was hurt to just hold tight. We'd have to wait away from the road and somebody would come by and find a way to get our van off of the barrier. Of course, though, it wasn't our van.

I decided to call Johnny right away while the adrenaline was still pumping around my body, and while I was looking at the van in a sorry state. Johnny didn't answer so I called Keith, the singer of Captain Black. He took it well - he was more concerned for our safety rather than the van. More bad news came, though: the van only had third-party fire and theft insurance. That meant it wasn't covered for our accident. The van looked like a right-off. I promised Keith that I would sort it out. I had no idea how, but I promised that somehow I'd make it okay. I'm not sure if he believed me or not.

We waited in the rain watching cars fly by for over an hour. We were soaked through and time was ticking by. How long did stuff like that take? Even when they got the van off it was not going to drive anywhere. What about the big gig? I was supposed to be at the venue for soundcheck and it started to look like I was going to miss that. Ally suggested I go for it. He'd look after the van situation so that I could find a way of getting into town. Like I said, the guy's a legend. I didn't know exactly where we were but I knew we must have been on the edge of London somewhere. We hugged again. I grabbed my guitar and walked off down the hard shoulder.

Motorways are not designed for pedestrians. I had to scramble up the side of a bridge that led to a dual carriageway. I walked along the side of that for a bit then I found an industrial estate. I went in and asked for directions to a train station, a cab rank, whatever really, just some kind of transport. Seemed we were further out than I thought. It was a forty minute walk to the nearest train station and nobody knew a taxi number. I had my phone but this predated Google Maps, Uber and all that jazz. Not that they would have done me any good anyway. I went to call the tour manager to explain I was going to be late and I that I would probably miss soundcheck but that I'd make the show. My phone was dead. Shit. Nothing I could do. I walked on.

I like to think of myself as a reliable person. Of all my years of playing shows, I've never knowingly missed a gig. I've had to cancel one or two due to illness. I've also had double bookings or changes in schedule that meant pulling shows, but not many, and I've played a fuck load of shows. One thing I would never do is just not show up for a gig. In fact, the only time anything like that had ever happened was in Glasgow at the start of that very tour. I was forgiven due to the confusion but if I didn't show up for the Hammersmith gig, without any word of warning, I may as well have just died in the crash.

I squeezed myself through the London rush hour and made it to Hammersmith just before doors opened. Kate, the band and crew, were all sat down for dinner backstage as I fell into the room, soaking wet, out of breath and rushing.

"I'm sorry I'm late. I was in a car crash!" I didn't have anytime to explain more than that. I needed to get my shit ready. I had a gig to play. At Hammersmith fucking Apollo. I tuned up, was given the thumbs up and I stepped on stage. The place was huge. The audience cheered.

"I AM ALIVE."

~

That would be a nice way to wrap this story up, going full circle right back to the start, but we can't do that now can we? Ally was still left in the rain on the side of the M3 with a totalled van that I'd promised to replace, repair or make good in some way or another.

I spoke to Ally after the show. Apparently they'd had to close the M3 and bring in a mini crane in order to lift the van from the crash barrier. It took a while and definitely did even more damage to the van. He signed up to the AA who came to the rescue and got the van on a flatbed truck and took it to a local garage in Holloway.

It turned out the van wasn't an absolute right off, but it was going to cost seven hundred pounds to fix it. Even though it was only worth around eight-hundred pounds, getting it fixed was the cheapest option, so it's the one I went for. I wasn't the sort of person to have that sort of cash lying around, though. Nor could I get my hands on it anytime soon.

This was while Nambucca was in full swing. Ally and I both lived there. Ally was, and still is, a brilliant promoter and I know a few things about organising gigs and parties. What the hell, we thought. Let's do a charity gig. Van Aid was born. We figured we could do an all-dayer the following Saturday and try to get a bunch of bands to play. We could do a little door cover and pass the buckets around - see if we could raise enough money to fix the van up. Seven hundred pounds felt like a lot to make on one event but it was our only real option.

We got on the phone and rang the best bands that we knew. Ringing someone out of the blue and telling them you'd recently been involved in a high speed crash on a motorway has quite a shocking effect. It seemed that if you hit them up with the idea of playing a free show the following weekend they would be up for it. It was very humbling because pretty much everyone we asked said yes and before we knew it we had a full bill of some fucking incredible bands. At the time, many of these acts were new and playing pub gigs but many would go on to do great things. Looking back on that all-dayer, we actually booked a festival line-up that would be recognised the world over. It featured Mumford and Sons, Dan Smith (of Bastille), Frank Turner, Soko, Eliza Doolittle, The Noisettes, SixNationState and, of course, Captain Black. I had a huge piece of paper pinned up behind the bar with the seven hundred pounds target to get the van fixed and I'd update it on the hour so everyone knew how close we were.

It goes without saying that the day was a blast, full of musical collaborations, brilliant shows and three stages in a pub that normally has one. It was rammed and the target was smashed.

With the left-over money we said we'd pay any speeding fines or parking tickets for anyone at the show. If they brought them to the pub within a week, we'd pay them off.

We counted up the cash and it was presented on stage, school fete, charity-style back to Keith, Johnny and Captain Black. Keith said I could crash his van whenever I wanted. Ally and I hugged and the mission was complete.

Another band that played that day, a late edition that got in contact once the show was announced, was called Handshake. A London based, seven-piece, instrumental folk band. They played danceable, traditional bangers full of fiddle, harmonica, and accordion. Brilliant players, all of them. While watching them, an old mate, and another Nambucca resident, Andy Peyton, said "You should get these as your backing band."

Backing band. What the fuck was he on about? I was solo musician. I didn't need no backing band!

The thought stayed with me, though, and a couple of years later, after I'd released my first record, I was thinking about my second and it came to mind again. Since Van Aid, Handshake had played a few more shows at venues I was working at (by then, Nambucca had gone up in smoke) and I'd become friends with them. I met up with Bob and Beth for a pint and put forward my suggestion. Did they wanna come on board for the summer? They could play back-up for my songs and then jump into a studio and make a record. I told them that, where possible, I'd help get Handshake their own gigs at the festivals as well. They said yes and that's exactly what we did. We had a great summer and followed it up by making my second record, 'Writing on the Wall'.

Asking people to play as a backing band for a summer is one thing. There was little to no money in it, especially for seven people. However, festival tickets and good shows, plus the chance to get Handshake's name out a bit, was enough to make it work. I knew full well that the band wouldn't be able to commit to anymore than that. It's not like they'd all be up for trekking around the country to get paid twenty pounds to play for twenty people. At the time, that was the reality of a tour I was hoping to put together. I did think that maybe Bob would be up for it, though. I'd become close with the whole band over the summer, but especially Bob. He was the banjo player and for one of the weekends over the summer the rest of the band couldn't make it, but Bob could. He suggested we do it as a duo. Musically, it worked really well and with just two people the logistics of a tour looked a bit more realistic - so I asked Bob if he fancied coming on tour.

Something of a love affair was born. We've never been physical but we've shared many a bed, many a hotel room, many long drives, many drinks, laughs and songs together. We've travelled the world and we've pretty much talked about everything there is to talk about. It takes a special kind of friendship for two people to do a ten thousand mile drive around the USA and we have that. He's been involved in every record I've made since. He was one of the best men at my wedding (I had three, because why the fuck not?) and he arranged for my wife and father-in-law to be driven to the ceremony in a vintage Rover. That's the kind of guy he is. Thanks, Bobby Banjo, you legend.

So, there we go. That story kind of went all over the place. I'm not sure if it's even supposed to have a moral. Maybe don't wash your hair? Or don't wear your seatbelt? Maybe it's worth taking a punt and doing a random holiday alone. In a roundabout way, you may end up with a new pal.

RAGE

2008 was the last time I went to Reading festival. It was the year Rage Against the Machine were playing as part of a big comeback tour. I was also playing. My show was on the Alternative Stage. It was a small stage that had comedy, talks and random bits and bobs going on, along with the odd musical act. That was my second year playing at Reading but I'd been attending the festival for years.

To say I was a regular at Reading is an understatement. After that first Glasto trip in 1997, I dragged a bunch of mates along to Reading Festival. It was much easier to get to from Essex - a hell of a lot harder to sneak in to, but not impossible. It was like Glastonbury's angry teenage brother. Rammed to the rafters with kids away from their parents for the first time, experimenting with drink, drugs and each other. I fucking loved it. It was also very much about the music. There were incredible lineups on stages that were very close to each other. You could (and I did) leg it around all day watching up to twenty world-class bands in an afternoon. At night, it would descend into a Lord of the Flies style carnage of fires, fights, and tomfoolery. There were less free hugs than Glasto but still a sense of unity, freedom, and adventure. I went every single year.

Many moons later, during the FROG days, I started working with the festival. FROG was held in one of The Mean Fiddler's venues in London's West End. At the time, The Mean Fiddler were one of the country's biggest music promoters and they ran Reading and Leeds. The Reading festival is held on the edge of Reading Town Centre. It's on a sports ground and at the entrance to the site is The Rivermead Sports Centre. As part of the festival, they would hold big welcome parties in the sports hall on the Thursday night. They were generally run by the hip club promoters of the time and, for a short spell, that was us.

It was a sweet deal. We had minimal budget but were given a fuck load of tickets. Something stupid like forty guest tickets in exchange for decking out the venue and playing some tunes. We could do that with our eyes closed. We gave people tickets to flyer and we took the extended FROG family down to Reading for the weekend to cause mayhem. Once the party was thrown on the Thursday, we were all free for the weekend. We had nice guest camping tickets, backstage access and the like.

At this time, I'd only just started playing as Beans on Toast. I had played the open mic show at Glastonbury that I've told you about, but I was a long way off from actually getting properly booked to play at any festivals. I was yet to release my first album; it was very early doors.

I also had a bit of a thing for graffiti at the time - and that's putting it lightly. The correct term for it would probably be bombing or tagging. That's the art of writing the same thing fucking everywhere. Beans on Toast, in my handwriting, was my tag. You could call it a logo but I say tag. I'd also say tagging is a pretty reasonable response to all the logos we're forced to endure on a daily basis. Logo, logo, logo (I'd actually read Naomi Klein's amazing 'No Logo' a few years prior which was definitely a turning point for me in how I viewed the world). If you've got loads of dosh you pay for a marketing campaign and plaster your logo where people will see it so you can sell them your shit. If you're skint, you get a marker pen and do pretty much the same thing, even if you have nothing to sell. I'd tagged a few toilets at the last Glasto I'd been to and a few people had commented saying that they'd seen it. One of these led to a gig so it seemed like a good way to get the word around and maybe get a few gigs at the same time.

The second year that we threw the 'Welcome to Reading Party', I took my marker pen and went to town. If you're going to do it, do it properly. And I did. The first night I did every bin on site. We're talking hundreds of bins. They were big green plastic wheelie bins and it was extremely effective as they were all over the main arena, campsite, and surrounding car parks. After that, I continued my assault on tent walls, tables, poles, and of course toilets. I've got a weak bladder at the best of times and being at a festival drinking white lightning by the three-litre bottle opens up the floodgates. I made sure I didn't have a piss without leaving my name on the toilet wall. I'll admit to you now, it got out of hand.

I woke up on the Sunday to a phone call from a friend who worked at The Mean Fiddler. He explained he'd just come out of a security meeting that was called solely to discuss 'Beans on Toast'. Nobody within The Mean Fiddler knew me as Beans on Toast at this time, just as Jay the promoter of FROG. Thankfully, there was no obvious connection apart from this mate. He wasn't going to grass me up but he warned me I was in the shit. Big time. I then found out my friend Dan had been nicked. I'd tagged his white T-shirt and when security saw it, they presumed he'd been tagging the site. He had his wristband cut off and was marched to the police compound where he was interrogated for two hours. Of course, he explained that he'd just found the shirt on the floor and had no idea what they were on about (always choose your friends wisely). The police told him I'd caused ten thousand pounds worth of damage. I now know that's bullshit but, as I said, it got well out of hand. It got even worse when my friend

Anastasia was cornered by security. She was wearing some (very sexy) short shorts and I'd tagged her leg with the Beans on Toast tag disappearing underneath them. She's a good friend and it was hilarious at the time but when she was questioned by security, rather than grass me up, she said that she was asleep when it was written and she had no idea who did it. All of a sudden I was assaulting young girls as well.

I toned it down a bit but continued to tag throughout the day. While everyone was running around looking for me, I was actually sat having lunch with the festival organisers who were praising me for doing such a good job of the warm-up party. They said we'd be invited back the following year for sure. The festival wrapped up and off home we went. I'd got away with it and so had my mates who'd been dragged into it. For a record label it would have been a dream marketing campaign and it definitely helped get the name out there. Every now and then people still bring it up. Even if they've seen or heard nothing since, I'll be introduced to someone as Beans on Toast and they'll say - didn't you pull that graffiti stunt at Reading Festival? That's pretty mad seen as it was over ten years ago.

The best thing to come from it, though, was about six months later when the main booker of the festival got in touch. Once again, I knew him from FROG. He said "Jay, if I book you to play Reading this year, will you leave your marker pen at home?"

That's how I got my first gig at Reading.

My first show at Reading in 2007 went well. I was so excited to be playing the festival I'd been attending for so long. As agreed, my pen stayed at home. I was on my best behavior and was invited back the following year. That was the year that Rage played.

Rage walked onto the stage wearing bright orange Guantanamo Bay jumpsuits, fully equipped with black hoods and hand ties. They walked out and stood on stage in silence before their set, making a profound political statement before they kicked in with the music. To be honest, I found the stunt a bit naff. They didn't follow it up with any talk or information about Guantanamo Bay, or suggest any ways to help. They just did the suit bit then cracked on with the set.

Rage are obviously an incredible band. They're one of the greatest and what they have done to enliven, enrich, encourage and entertain the masses is undeniable. So, for a fool like me to sit here criticising them is dumb, but at the time, I just found it a bit crass. I've never really been a fan of comeback or reunion tours and that's what this was. It just struck me as "fuck you I won't tidy my bedroom" rather than "fuck you I won't do what you tell me." But what do I know? I watched a few tunes and in the end belted off to watch a new act I'd heard about. They were called Dan Le Sac and Scroobius Pip and they enraged, encouraged and entertained me greatly.

That night, at Reading, I was having a wild one. At some point, walking past one of the many festival clothes stalls, I saw a bright orange jumpsuit. It wasn't exactly Guantanamo Bay but it wasn't far off. As soon as I laid eyes on it, I knew exactly what I had to do.

Reading has a sister festival in Leeds that aptly goes by the name 'Leeds'. It runs on the same weekend and has the same lineup. Part and parcel of playing Reading is that you play Leeds as well - the same for me and the same for Rage. That meant that the following day I'd be playing in the afternoon (on the tiny Alternative Stage) before they'd take to the (Main) stage that evening.

My plan was that the following day in Leeds, at 1pm in the afternoon, I'd walk on stage wearing a bright orange jumpsuit with a hood over my head and proclaim that I was making a 'profound political statement'. Everyone would think I was a fucking idiot but later that night, when they all went to see Rage, who would also make the same profound political statement, it wouldn't seem crass. It would seem deep and meaningful, and more importantly, I'd no longer be a fucking idiot - I'd be a bloody genius.

The plan was flawless. I bought the jumpsuit.

The wild night continued well into the morning and most of the long drive to Leeds (with Stretch in the transit putting up with my drunken nonsense). I fell asleep for a few, quick hours before we got to Leeds. I was a bit wobbly but nothing a quick line of gak wouldn't sort out. I had my orange suit ready to roll and the plan was to tell no one about the Rage jumpsuit thing. I'd just do it and fuck off straight back off to Reading. All would be revealed later, and we'd be long gone. It would be hilarious.

This was a time when I used to stand on chairs at gigs. That's a story for another time. But every gig I played, I'd stand on a chair or a bar stall. Or, if there was something taller, then I'd stand on that. It was a thing. It turned out one of the stage crew at Leeds was a mate, or at least knew about the standing on things thing, and she'd prepared a little treat for me. She'd put a hard case for a huge bass amp in the center of the stage. It was massive, with a mic stand and DI (where I plug in my guitar) on the top. It looked stupid: it was perfect. She'd also put a few stage blocks leading up to the top so it should be easy enough to climb. Or at least that was the plan.

It also turned out I was playing just before the legend that is Henry Rollins. He was doing a spoken word set, telling stories and sharing his brilliant mind with the world. People were so excited about it that they came early. The tent was rammed. I wasn't really expecting much of a crowd so it was incredible for me. Especially as I thought that Henry Rollins fans had got to be up for a profound political statement or two.

I did a few lines, necked half a bottle of white lightning and put on my orange suit. I hadn't managed to find a proper hood, but I had a black bin liner. I did try to cut a small eye hole but didn't want to spoil the effect. I was just trying to work out how I was going to see out when I got the thumbs up. It was stage time.

As I'm sure you can imagine, it was a bit of a shambles. I can't tell you what I looked like because I couldn't see a thing. It was completely pitch black. I was trying to clamber up a bunch of stage blocks to stand on top of the bass case. It took me five minutes to get up there but when I did, I shouted "I'm making a profound political statement!" Again, I've no idea how the crowd reacted. I actually half choked on the bin liner and it took me ages to rip it off my head. Then I was way too hot in the suit and I had to get it off - that took a while as well. I was ten minutes into my twenty-five minute set before I'd even played one song. I looked like an absolute tit to a massive crowd, but I didn't care. I knew all along that later that night, when Rage went on stage, everyone would get it. It would be legendary.

I squeezed as much as possible into my next fifteen minutes. I got off the stage, high-fived Henry Rollins, got in the van and headed back for another wild night at Reading. I'd only let one person in on the joke: my mate Ollie Russian who was at Leeds for the weekend. I'd told him that Rage were going to do the same thing that evening and to go check it out. He also agreed it was worth losing half the set for a gag that good.

We arrived back at Reading that evening. Just as we were pulling in, Ollie sent me a text. Rage had their set cut short. They didn't do the Guantanamo Bay Jumpsuit thing.

I'm yet to be invited back to Reading or Leeds.

INTERVAL
GERMAN MONSTER STORIES

Presumably, you're reading this in chronological order. If that's correct, then we're now around the halfway point. Well done.

I may or may not have already mentioned this but I'm writing the majority of this book whilst travelling around Germany on trains. I've heard some fantastic monster stories whilst I've been here. In light of that, I thought I'd step away from the self-indulgence and share a couple with you. Just as a little interval. I have also decided against checking the facts of these stories so this is just what I have been told by local, drunk people late at night...

The Monster of Aachen
The monster of Aachen looks a bit like a tiger but bigger - about twice the size, in fact. It's jet black and has a huge lizard-like tail and giant sharp fangs. He is undoubtedly a scary motherfucker. He is, however, not your everyday monster. The monster of Aachen is something of a vigilante. As legend would have it, late at night the monster attacks drunk men who have been cheating on their wives. He is, ladies and gentlemen, a monster with morals - morals that I agree with. Aachen was the first stop on the tour. I pride myself on being a faithful and monogamous husband, but when I had the opportunity to go and visit the monster on the first day of a tour, well, I figured it wouldn't hurt. Obviously, it's near

impossible to lay eyes on the actual thing but, as a reminder to the town, they have a statue of the monster just outside the town square. En route to the gig, we went to check it out. It turns out they were doing some heavy construction work above the statue. In order to preserve the statue, and keep it safe, they put some scaffolding around it, effectively caging the beast. What this means, I don't know. Perhaps while the monster is caged, the drunken fools of Aachen are out running amok. Of course, I did my best to free the monster, but the scaffolding was pretty tight and I had a gig to play.

The Monster of Hannover

Hannover is famous for a brand of cookies. The actual brand name escapes me now but it's a buttery, sugary treat. A yellow square with cute, little rippled edges. It's Hannover's finest export and is enjoyed throughout Germany and the world. The biscuit makers HQ and baking factory are both in the town centre, and above the door to the HQ, there is a giant golden cookie. Or at least there was. A few years back, Hannover woke up to find the cookie had vanished overnight. The town and company were both confused and outraged until that afternoon when a letter and photograph were sent to both the cookie makers and the local press. The photo was of the cookie monster (as in Sesame Street's finest) with the golden cookie in his mouth. The letter was written in classic ransom note style: words haphazardly cut out from magazines and newspapers. It said something along the lines of "I'm the cookie monster. I've got your golden cookie. I'll give it back to you but only after you've given every child in the local children's hospital free cookies." Fucking brilliant! More vigilante monsters. The press went nuts as did the rest of town. The cookie monster went from being a thief to an instant hero. By making the robbery selfless and hilarious, the monster turned

61

the whole thing on its head. The company did the only thing it could do and dished out free cookies to all the kids in the hospital. The cookie was returned the following day. It was found hanging around the neck of a statue in the town centre and the cookie monster was never heard of again. I'm not even sure if the police even bothered to launch an investigation. The cookie monster had won and the kids got free biscuits.

Anyway, enough about great German monsters. Where was I…

THE FUNNIEST THING
I EVER SAID

The funniest thing that I ever said was at a festival called "Endorse It In Dorset". Cleverly, it was situated in Dorset and it was very much a Dorset festival with cider drinkers, punks, travellers, farmers and music lovers. Think Pronghorn or Dreadzone as headliners. It was brilliant.

It was my first time attending and I was working for Strummerville who were running a small area within the festival. As usual, we had a massive campfire. By that campfire, we had a small vocal PA so bands could play next to the fire and we decorated the whole area with fairy lights, bunting and loads of sofas. We also had Joe Strummer's old flags. He had collected flags from around the world over the years and strung them together like giant bunting as a symbol of unity and togetherness. Whenever we did a fire, we'd put as many of the flags up as possible. There were so many of them that we rarely managed to fly them all. This time around we had nowhere near enough flagpoles which was a shame, but we put up all that we could. They looked amazing and it always felt like an honour, both hanging them and just being part of the fire over the weekend.

I'm not going to lie. It was quite a debauched festival. We had loads of crew and not a huge amount to do so everybody just got bang on it and had a blast. It was my job to look after the fire and PA for the graveyard shift 4am - 10am. Not a huge amount would happen. I'd put blankets over the folks who'd crashed out on the sofas, stopped the really hammered ones from jumping into the fire, and I kept the fire burning and the firewood stocked.

I started doing this thing called 'Breakfast with Beans on Toast'. Around 5am I'd set up the PA, plug in and start to sing to whoever was left around the fire. This would generally be a small handful of people. There were some gurning folk still buzzing from the night before, a few sleeping people, or those just chilling on the sofas and keeping warm. I'd keep it pretty quiet and low key but they were fun shows, and with nothing else going on or even open across the whole site, I felt like we were providing a good service for the festival.

It was also a good time for me to try out new songs and I played one I'd just written called "Dirty Paki". It is an anti-racist song about togetherness and unity but it says a lot of stupid shit in it. By singing small-minded, racist, sexist and bigoted comments, I was hoping to shine a light on the stupidity of racism and then follow it up with a chorus about unity - why we shouldn't be scared of each other. It's a list of the world's worst taboos - that gay people have aids, or that people who work in kebab shops are terrorists. I'm sure you know the kind of mind-numbingly, moronic ignorance I'm referring to. In fact, the opening line of the song contains the word 'paki'. I'd like to think that anyone who knows me or my music would get where I was coming from. Anyone hearing it for the first time would have to listen to it all the way through and hopefully not shut off after hearing the harsh words. My plan would normally be to have a bit of a chat about the song before I played it, telling people to hold tight and not judge it until the chorus. I'd also make it clear that it was an anti-racism song from the off. That didn't matter this time, though, because from what I could see, nobody was listening. There were just some sleeping bods or a few folks that were only half paying attention. I was actually a bit surprised when a few claps came my way after the song. The gig then carried on and a few more people joined us as they either woke up or headed from a party they were having in a tent or car park somewhere. I played a few more tunes then wrapped it up. I stuck the iPod on with an old Trojan Reggae compilation and was waiting out the rest of my shift before I could get some kip.

I saw him coming a mile off. A skinhead in a bomber jacket bowling towards the fire. He looked pissed off and I decided to keep my eye on him. One of my job descriptions was to keep the peace and something about this dude gave me the feeling he had a different job description altogether. He walked straight up to the fire and up to some skinny, little indie kid who'd been up all night and wasn't in the place for any kind of confrontation and said "Who was singing the songs about pakis?" It was loud enough for everyone sat around the fire to hear.

I stood up and walked over, hoping to bring the level of conversation down a bit and said

"Oh hi. I was the one singing earlier. What's up?"

"I'm with Bradford BNP." He said.

Oh shit. He didn't really say anything after that but I could tell he just wanted to find out more about the use of the word paki and hopefully find other people he could be mean, horrible and racist with.

I said "I'm with Strummerville and I think you may have misheard the song. It was an anti-racist song. Nobody here wants anything to do with the BNP or its beliefs in any way. In fact, quite the opposite." I pointed at the surroundings. "We're a bunch of people sat around a campfire at a music festival. What on earth makes you think we'd be racists?" I pointed to the flags. "We've got all the flags in the world hanging up around us."

He looked at the flags and said "you haven't got all the flags in the world."

And then I said "that's just cos we didn't have enough poles."

There was an odd silence as we looked at each other.

I, of course, meant flagpoles, but the way it came out sounded like I was referring to highly skilled Polish workers.

"That's pretty funny." I said. He started to laugh as well.

"Now, fuck off!" I said and pointed away from our fire.

Looking back, that was probably the most aggressive thing I'd ever said but I knew I needed rid of him. That was my job, after all. Thankfully, he walked away and we never heard from him again.

A few times since that event I've been questioned about the song, 'Dirty Paki'. Ninety-nine percent of the time people get my take on it but I have met a few people along the way that disagreed with it or felt that I'd approached the subject in the wrong way. If you're one of those people, I apologise. I understand that people feel uncomfortable when hearing such offensive phrases - I certainly do - but I thought that it was a good way to make people stop and think. It is quite a tricky subject to tackle but I'd rather try to tackle it than ignore it. I believe that by talking about these problems and addressing them, we can start to deal with them. I think we need to confront racism, sexism, and all the 'isms' by talking about them openly. I've never been one to ignore the elephant in the room. In fact, that's who I'm singing for a lot of the time. If I had the chance, I'd love to sing the song again for the chap from Bradford BNP. I'd like to get his take on it and talk it out, but it was 6am and we'd been up all night. I was satisfied with how the situation worked out: no anger, or violence, just a strangely unintentional, shit joke to get me and my fellow fire dwellers safely into the next day.

I still stand by the song and sing it regularly. I've also been telling this story when I've played the song over the years. I refer to it as "the funniest thing I ever said" but it's only really now that I'm writing it down that it seems ironic that the funniest thing I've ever said was actually a racist pun based on one of the generalisations I intended to criticise.

Talking of generalisations, why did I presume the skinhead was going to cause trouble just from taking one look at him? What does that say about me? Either way, I believe in equal rights. For me, it doesn't matter where you come from, what you look like, your gender, skin colour or sexuality etc. What matters is how you act and who you are.

"Let's sit on both sides of the fence. Where the grass is always green. If we forget about what we're scared about we might work out what we need."

THIS IS THE FISH

The first song I ever wrote was called 'Fish'. It was just a bunch of words and phrases thrown together. It wasn't about anything and bared no relation to me, my life, or the world around me. The chorus was the line 'This Is The Fish' repeated four times. I can't really remember how the whole song went now but I'm confident it was crap. However, I enjoyed the process of making something out of nothing and have been writing songs ever since. These days I'm lucky enough to make a living from the songs I write. I'd be hard pushed to call songwriting my profession as I've never really treated it like that, but it's certainly my trade. It's what I do.

Songwriting is a form of magic and one of its many powers is its ability to turn strangers into friends. As you've seen from the pages of this book, time and time again people have gone out of their way to help me while I travel around and play my music. The level of hospitality I've witnessed the world over is outrageous, and I wouldn't be able to do what I do without it. This magic is particularly strong within the songwriting community. The camaraderie amongst songwriters is a beautiful thing to behold, certainly the songwriters I've crossed paths with anyway. The opportunities I've been given by other musicians has been completely invaluable.

For me, songwriting goes around in circles. I write a song, the song ends up taking me somewhere interesting, which, in turn, inspires me to write another song - and round and round we go.

I realised this a few years back whilst snorkelling. I met eyes with a brightly coloured, tropical fish. The fish and I had a bit of a moment looking into each other's eyes and that first song came back to me. "This Is The Fish" I thought, and it occurred to me just how far my songs have taken me. Because I have to say, the last place that I ever thought I'd end up off the back of my three-chord ditties was on a cruise ship bound for the Bahamas.

It was 2015 and I was aboard 'Flogging Molly's Salty Dog Cruise'.

Back in my DJ days at sTatiK, one of my regular party tunes to drop was 'Drunken Lullabies' by Flogging Molly. To tell the truth, apart from that tune, I didn't really know much about the band, but it was a sure-fire Celtic folk banger. I saw the band for the first time many years later at The Cardiff Motorpoint Arena.

It was the first day of an arena tour opening for Frank Turner. I'd recently opened up Frank's first-ever arena show at Wembley - a prestigious day for Frank and everyone involved, and it really took things to the next level. I did my best to treat it like a normal gig, well a normal gig to ten thousand people anyway. I had a great twenty-minute opening set. I wrote a song ('Hello Wembley') especially for it and wrapped the whole thing up by crowd surfing the length of the arena. After the gig, Frank deemed me "arena ready" and when he booked his first arena tour, I was invited along. It was seven dates. I was opening and Flogging Molly were the main support. We were hitting up some of the UK's biggest venues - MEN in Manchester, Nottingham Arena and the like. It was wrapping up in London's O2. Fuck, yeah!

After my gig on the first night in Cardiff, Flogging Molly took to the stage. Dave King, the singer, went straight up to the mic and said "what about Beans on Toast? Isn't he just fucking brilliant?" The crowd cheered and then he said "now for something completely different" and the band kicked in - accordions, fiddles, whistles, banjo and punk rock for the next half an hour. I was mesmerised. What a show! I learned that the band that had been playing together for nineteen years and, fuck me, did it show. For a band that had been touring that long, they showed no sign of slowing down, both onstage and off. On the first night, I met the whole band over a few drinks. Following that, each night Dave said kind words about me to the arena crowds and each night they played a stomping set. At the Nottingham show, the full backdrop fell onto George the drummer and he didn't miss a beat. That's a ten feet long piece of heavyweight material falling on your head in the middle of a song - he just kept the beat going until someone pulled the bloody thing off. Incredible.

Flogging Molly's dressing room door was always wide open. Each time Bobby Banjo and I walked past, we'd be pulled in and given a Guinness. We'd talk about life, music and touring. They explained how they'd given Frank some of his early shows out in America because they loved his music so much, and how great it was to be playing arenas with him in the UK. We all became friends quickly. After the Manchester gig, there was an organised after-show party at the venue and everyone got shit-faced. It was there and then that a special friendship was born. It was born out of mutual respect, whiskey and the camaraderie I was talking about earlier.

Most nights of the tour, Bobby and I would play gigs outside the arenas as the venue was closing. This was a fun way to end the night and also a way of selling merchandise without paying the venue a cut of the cash. A couple of times, Nathan, Bob (Flogging Molly also have a banjo player called Bob) and Matt, also from the band, would come out and jam with us - just for the fuck of it. It was a short run but friendship grew deep and fast in a way that can only happen on tour. Towards the end of a drunken night, Nathan Maxwell, bass player extraordinaire, made what sounded like a drunken, momentary promise. If we ever made it out to America - didn't matter when and didn't matter where - as long as we could get to a Flogging Molly gig, we could open for them.

Little did he know (but I was pretty quick to tell him) that soon after the arena shows were done, Bobby and I were heading out to the States for a handful of headline shows. It was the first time we were doing our own shows in the USA and we had a few small venues booked up on the East Coast. We were doing Boston, New York and then a couple in Canada. Then it was back down to Chicago, Nashville, then looping back up to NYC. It was small but it was a start. We also had a few days off. It was a long shot but maybe Flogging Molly were playing somewhere on these days off. It turned out they had a run of US tour dates around the same time (I learned later that FM are always on tour). We put the dates next to each other and Nathan said it didn't look good. The closest show would mean a nine hour drive from NYC to Detroit to do one show opening for Flogging Molly. We'd then have to drive all the way back to Rochester, New York. It didn't make sense but Bobby and I didn't give a shit if it made sense or not. Was it possible? Yes, it was. Nathan seemed pleased with our blind eagerness. Right then and there we drunkenly shook hands and the gig was confirmed.

By the time I woke up the following day, I'd received an email from Flogging Molly's booking agent in the States. A contract, and the show information for our upcoming gig at 'The Fillmore' in Detroit, quickly followed. Nathan Maxwell, bass player of Flogging Molly, is a man of his word.

The tour finished at the O2 Arena in London, as promised. There were twenty thousand people and it was, by far, my biggest ever show. My soundcheck for this giant show in this prestigious venue clocked in at fifty-seven seconds. I remember this because we had an ongoing gag with the sound crew about doing the shortest soundcheck in the history of the building. I've never really been a fan of soundchecks and always keep them short and sweet - basically just checking that it all works. But, the funny thing is, the bigger the venues got, the easier soundchecks got. When the venues are big, you're touring with a team of professional sound crew who look after your sound every night. On that tour they were bringing the whole fucking PA with them - the same people were using the same equipment each night - just in a different building. Each night the soundchecks got shorter and shorter and, by London, someone had thrown down the gauntlet of sound-checking in under a minute. Fifty-seven seconds, mate. Smashed it!

The gig itself was next level. Whoever thought that I'd be playing in fucking arenas? I opened the set with a brand new love song about Lizzy that she'd not heard until that point. It seemed like an appropriate way of rising to the occasion.

In the blink of an eye the arenas were gone. I was a few dates into the American tour and staring down the barrel of our nine hour nonstop drive to Detroit. Actually, I wasn't. Bob was. I was drunk. We'd just played a show at Rockwood Music Hall, and, in order to make the show in Detroit, we needed to leave straight after the show and hit the road. I'm an awful driver and I never play gigs sober so I was allowed to drink at the show, safe in the knowledge that Bob would take the wheel. New York has a strange effect on me; I always seem to end up proper hammered – that night was no exception. I clambered into the car and passed out. When I woke, we were in Detroit. Thanks, Bob - you legend.

That was my first visit to the 'Motor City' but the idea of Detroit has always fascinated me. The little that I did know about the city I'd learnt from the Julian Temple documentary and '8 Mile'. It's true that the city is half empty and huge parts of it have been pretty much been left to rot. What was once the bright future of American Industry had become a window into a different, more bleak future of broken windows and abandoned buildings. But, in between the gaps, there was beauty and on top of everything, there was an incredible pride. That pride was displayed brilliantly on the T-shirt worn by the bouncer at the club. It said 'Detroit vs Everything'.

Flogging Molly's crowd was huge and amazingly welcoming. There was no way that any of those five thousand people who knew Bobby and I were when we hit the stage at The Fillmore. It was a beautiful venue in the heart of the city opposite Comerica Park baseball stadium. After thirty minutes, though, it felt like we'd made friends with every single member of the audience. Before I even had a chance to thank Nathan and the guys for having us play, they informed me that they wanted us to open up on more shows. They wanted to know if we could we make it to Texas rather than going back to the UK after our headline shows. Sure we could. They also wanted to know if we could then head to New Orleans for the tour finale. Yes we could and yes we would. At that moment, though, Nathan suggested we just enjoy Detroit in all its crazy beauty and that's what we did.

The name Beans on Toast means very little in America. Across the pond, it's not seen as a solid, affordable and tasty snack - most Americans have never even heard of it. They have baked beans. Yeah. And toast. But they don't eat them together. To an American it just sounds like a stupid idea. For that reason, I often find myself explaining my choice of name. To simplify it, I generally tell them that it would be like an American calling themselves 'Hotdog'.

This was how I met Josef Coney Island. As I explained this to Josef, who was working on the stage crew that night, he told me that in Detroit, a 'Coney Island' was a special form of local hotdog. He also told me that he was a rapper that went by the name of said hotdog. So, we were both hotdogs. After he watched the show, he decided we were like musical cousins and we did the only logical thing to do: we went to get a Coney Island from downtown Detroit.

That's one of the real gems of touring. If I visit a city for the first time and I don't have a gig, I never really know where to go. I just end up doing obvious tourist crap and drinking in the obvious tourist bars. Therefore, local knowledge is priceless and generally hard to come by - unless you're playing a gig, of course. If you're playing a gig, it's always easy to get someone who knows the city to show you around, skipping past the bullshit and straight to the nooks and crannies, which seem to be my favourite parts. So, after the show was wrapped up, and the stage was cleared, we climbed into Josef's ride and took off for a real tour of Detroit and a late night hotdog.

Seen by some as a pretty hardcore area of Detroit, Josef was born and raised in the Hamtramck. He knew, like all other out of towners, that what we would want to do was check out some 'urban porn'. So, with a belly full of hotdogs, he drove us through a maze of abandoned derelict buildings. It really was quite something. He was so confident of empty roads that he would drive full speed through red light after red light, which was scary as fuck. We ended up at his Aunt's bar in Hamtramck, where we scored another gig.

Bob and I then headed back to our own tour, and so commenced a blur of house parties in Rochester, mountain climbing in Vancouver, rap battles in Chicago, bowling in St Louis, traffic jams in Nashville and cheesesteaks in Philly. Then we looped back up for another show in New York. It was quite eventful. New York was originally where the tour was going to end but Nathan Maxwell was a man of his word and, as promised, it had been arranged that we flew to Texas for another couple of shows with Flogging Molly, and then to New Orleans. All the shows were mind-blowing! This was especially true of the one in New Orleans. The gig was at The House of Blues whose stage had been blessed by every musical icon ever (as far as I could tell from the backstage graffiti). After the New Orleans show, there was an end-of-tour party at a nearby bar. It was there that Nathan first mentioned the cruise. The band were in talks of taking over a cruise ship in March the following year. They would run a festival on the boat as it shipped three thousand people to the Bahamas and back. The plan was to have gigs on the boat while it was moving. After telling us this, he said "you guys should come and play." Yes, Nathan - we should! Where do we sign? He said to leave it with him and we ventured out into the wild streets of New Orleans to lose our way.

New Orleans was the last night of the tour so it seemed only right to hang around for a few days and get stuck into the city before flying back to London. One of the only downsides of touring is sometimes places flash by in front of your eyes. Therefore, when opportunities to stay put for a few days come up, you take them. Also, when we announced the show in New Orleans, I got a message from a friend of a friend offering us somewhere to stay. That friend of a friend was Spider Stacy of The Pogues.

I am a huge Pogues fan (like anyone with a heart and a flair for the fantastic). I love them. I'd briefly met Spider through my work with Strummerville, and earlier with The Holloways, but that's not how he knew of me. A good friend of mine, Scampi Dan, played trumpet for The Pogues for many years. Dan plays a bit of trumpet with me from time to time and has since produced one of my albums, 'A Spanner in the Works'. It was through this that Spider had heard my music. I can only guess he liked it as he offered us a place to stay the minute I posted about the New

Orleans show - again demonstrating the camaraderie of a touring musician. So, as the tour ended, we were welcomed into the house of a personal hero who had an incredible wealth of local knowledge. Spider and his wife, Louise, lived in the Tremé area of New Orleans. Spider had been welcomed into the community, big time. He'd taken on a role in a TV show by the creator of 'The Wire'. It was called 'Tremé' – you've probably heard of it. It was all about the area and how in dealt with the after-effects of Hurricane Katrina. I'm not sure if it was his role in the show, his role in The Pogues, or the fact he's an all-round nice guy, but Spider was loved in New Orleans. Due to that, Bob and I felt very looked after. He also pointed us towards all the best spots for food, music, and dancing.

To say that New Orleans had an impact on me is an understatement. It's a city like no other. I remember clearly having a moment to myself on the banks of the Mississippi. I was really missing Lizzy; I'd been away for quite a while and the city reminded me of her - oysters, Bloody Marys, the music, and the dancing. I kept thinking that she'd love it there. It was there, by the river, that I decided I was going to ask Lizzy to marry me. I would then take her back to New Orleans (providing she said yes, of course). I found the perfect engagement ring in a little jewellery shop on Royal Street. We bid America farewell and headed back to Blighty.

Lizzy said yes.

Bob and I got stuck into a busy summer of UK festivals and started to put a plan together for our next trip to the States the following year. The plan was to hit up some of the places we'd played on our last tour and then gig our way down the East Coast so that we ended in Florida to climb on board the cruise ship.

At some point over the summer, the cruise was announced. The rumours were true. It was called 'The Salty Dog Cruise' and promised three days of punk rock on the open waters with free booze and free food for all. The lineup was incredible. Frank was playing, as was Gogol Bordello, Mariachi El Bronx, Morgan Heritage and a bunch of other amazing bands. One problem, though, Beans on Toast didn't appear to be on the lineup.

Shit.

Thinking back, I realised that the offer of the gig was made at the end of a huge tour in a bar in New Orleans. There's a good chance it got lost in the voodoo of it all. Nathan, and the Flogging Molly folks, had already done so much for me that I didn't want to push it too much. As the lineup was already announced, it felt like it might be cheeky to ask. But, that said, I'd kind of placed Bob and I in Miami for the correct date. Fuck it. I called Nathan. "Leave it with me." He said.

A few nervous months passed before I got a message from the band's agent in the States. I had two cabins, three gigs and a weekend of free booze and food on board 'The Salty Dog Cruise'. Shiver me timbers! Nathan came through again.

Now, when I say that I'd placed Bob and me in Miami for the correct day, this had not been an easy task. At that point in time, I could just about do my own shows in the bigger cities of the USA, as proven by the last tour. If I'd visited a city earlier with Frank (or now with Flogging Molly), it was worth heading back to play a small bar or club in town. There were some places, though, where there was no interest in booking a Beans on Toast show. But, with the help of the wonderful people at Xtra Mile Recordings, a plan was put together to play a tour of house concerts.

House concerts are what you would imagine from the name. A kind stranger opens up their house for the night and you play a gig there. The audience is usually comprised of their friends or, indeed, other strangers. They're generally small gatherings without PA or a bar. It strips a gig back to a very simple evening. You take a few beers and sit around and listen to some songs. You don't need many people to make these work so the plan was to join the dots - we'd do shows in bigger cities and some house concerts in between. That was yet another fine example of generosity. People were opening doors to us and these were front doors to people's living rooms in the suburbs of Washington, Atlanta, Gainesville, and the like. In general, we'd be fed, watered and offered a bed by these kind folks. After the gig, we'd pass around a tip jar that would get us petrol to the next show. The magic in full effect. It's a wonderful thing to be part of.

It was off the back of these heartwarming house gigs that we got to Miami. The boat was huge. In fact, it was fucking massive, way bigger than I had imagined, and it had shit loads of bars, restaurants, swimming pools and hot tubs. There were three inside venues and a stage out on the deck overlooking one of the pools. Not only that, there was also three thousand excitable punks all climbing aboard - Bob and I included. Beans on Toast was never actually added to the lineup, or announced as playing as such, but we had shows every day and I was fucking excited. Kitted out in a brand new Hawaiian shirt, Bermuda shorts and cheap sunglasses, I was ready.

The ship was leaving Miami on the Friday for an evening of gigs. We'd be docking at Nassau the following day to spend the day on the island, which is the capital of The Bahamas. Then, we'd be back onto the ship for more gigs. The next day we'd dock on a private island where Flogging Molly would play on a sunny beach before one more night of gigs on the boat. Then we'd return to Miami on Monday morning. It was like a holiday, a festival, a party and a concert all rolled into one - at sea.

By the time the boat set sail that evening, more booze had been consumed than any average weekend away on a cruise ship. Things were bound to get messy. With our recent house gigs in mind, Bob and I devised a plan to set up some cabin gigs. We made a big poster that said 'Beans on Toast - Gig in Your Cabin' with instructions about how to arrange such a thing. For the next three days, in between our actual gigs (and the drinking, swimming, sunbathing and watching all the other acts), Bob and I would turn up and play cabin gigs for two or three people at a time. They had the same charm and feeling as the recent house gigs; they were nice and personal and we made a shit loads of friends very quickly. Our last gig of the weekend was on Sunday night and the turnout was huge. It felt like half the boat had turned up to see us play, which is quite an achievement for a band that wasn't even on the bill!

The magic was there that weekend. There was a community feeling. A togetherness. It felt like the lunatics had taken over the asylum and they were all the better for it. Maybe it was because punk rock on a cruise ship sounded like such a nonsense idea that it worked so well. I also think it was the connection between the bands and their fans that was at the heart of it. Following Flogging Molly's lead, every band got involved in the party. It wasn't bands on stage and in dressing rooms and everyone else watching. It was all at the same party, all having a great time, all in the same boat. I've always enjoyed a party and this one was really easy to enjoy - the weather, the music, the people, and the sheer insanity that I'd been invited along. I was drinking, dancing, making friends and making up songs. I think I even wrote a song about a waterslide at one point, and then came my meeting with the fish.

Monday rolled around and we disembarked the boat with killer hangovers. What an experience. Surely it was a once in a lifetime kind of experience, though? Apparently not. About a week later I got a call from Flogging Molly's manager, Dan. We'd met on the boat and had become friends. He's an absolute legend of a dude who'd worked with some incredible bands and artists. After the huge success of the first cruise, they wanted to announce the following year's lineup ASAP. Dan wanted to know if I could write a song about the cruise that would also announce next year's lineup, too. Then he explained that he wanted me to film myself with my 'cruise get up' on singing the song. Sure thing. Of course I could.

Hmmm, would I be on the line up by any chance?

Yes. Yes, I would.

I've since been back to the Bahamas on The Salty Dog Cruise three times and, even now, as I write this, I've been confirmed to go next year. Provided I play my cards right, the following year too. I've played alongside bands such as Rancid, Nofx, The Skatalites and many more. It's an absolute blast every time. I even took my Mum and Dad along last year.

Since then, I've also opened up a lot more shows for Flogging Molly. I've done this on both sides of the pond and I am now close with the whole band. Last year, I was talking with Nathan on the boat. I wanted to thank him again for being true to his word and inviting us along. Nathan explained to me that he's a fan of rebel music. He said that punk rock comes in many shapes and sizes and it's an attitude rather than any particular sound or look. So, when Dave King stepped to the mic in Cardiff three years prior and said "now for something completely different," he was right. The sound is different but perhaps it comes from a similar place. If not, it's certainly heading there.

See you on the high seas soon, Shipmates.

MY LAST E

The last E that I ever took was at a festival called Bonnaroo in Manchester, Tennessee. It was 2013. It was fun but it ended up being bit of a shit show for me. The plan looked phenomenal on paper but you know how it goes with these things sometimes.

I was in the States touring with Frank Turner. It was my first proper tour out there - a two week run starting in Pennsylvania and ending at Bonnaroo. I was riding on the bus with Frank and The Sleeping Souls, playing huge sold-out shows, and getting to see parts of America I didn't even know existed. I was also getting to see places I recognised from Hollywood movies or country songs or Tom Robbins novels. Touring America gives you a real feel for 'the road' and all the old songs about it. It's such a huge place that it feels like you could just tour forever. You could rock up into town, play the gig and then disappear off into the sunset. Doing it on a full-blown tour bus ('Almost Famous' style) was a dream of mine - and probably anyone who ever wrote a song. I realised just how lucky I was to be doing it. Thanks, Frank. You bloody legend.

Frank's tour finished up with him playing at Bonnaroo festival. He was heading in to play his show and then straight away he and his band were all leaving to start a European tour. I, on the other hand, had nothing planned after the tour. I could get into

Bonnaroo on Frank's bus and although I didn't actually have a gig at the festival, I had every intention of hanging out for the weekend and seeing how the Americans partied in a field.

Leading up to the tour, I started trying to blag shows at the festival. I found a contact for a chap that ran a solar-powered stage that promoted social change through music. I sent some tunes and info about myself, along with UK festival shows and adventures. He took a bit of convincing but as I didn't need a ticket, nor money, nor hospitality of any kind, I persuaded him to give me a thirty-minute slot.

As mentioned, Frank was leaving site after his gig. I'd just finished a tour overseas so there was no way in the world I would have a tent or any kind of festival essentials on me. You might, therefore, be wondering why I would claim that I didn't need hospitality. Well, this was the second half of my master plan. That year's festival headliners, and by far the biggest band in America at that time, happened to be my old pals, Mumford and Sons.

I've already mentioned that Mumford played some early shows at Nambucca. I, like everyone else who saw them in those early days, was absolutely blown away and went to many gigs that they played in and around London. It was clear from the off that they were destined for great things. I think it was 'The River Rat Pack Tour' that really cemented our friendship. The brainchild of Ally Wolf, Nat Jenkins and myself, 'The River Rat Pack' was a musical escapade on the waterways between London and Oxford. Five bands on three barges that move just a bit faster than walking speed. We'd take a week to do a journey that would take two hours in a car. Every night, usually by the water's edge, we played gigs in pubs. The turnout for the shows was never huge but there was something very special about those tours. Everyone was crammed into three tiny boats and we were all sleeping in shifts in and around the constant partying and making of music. Lifelong friendships were born on those barges. I'm yet to do another tour where more music was played off stage than on, and collaborations certainly came thick and fast. The tour ran for three years with some of the finest musicians I've ever played with. Mumford and Sons were on the first ever RRP Tour and we've been friends ever since. Ben Lovett produced my first album, 'Standing on a Chair', and the band have invited me to play at some incredible shows and festivals over the years.

So, in the lead up to Bonnaroo, I gave the lads a shout. Explaining that I was coming into the festival, I told them I was keen to hang out but I wouldn't have anywhere to stay. They said it was no problem. They had my back. I could stay with them.

In fact, they said that after Bonnaroo, they were driving (also in a dream tour bus) to a bluegrass festival in Telluride, Colorado. Did I wanna tag along, they asked? Fuck, yeah. I did. They even said they could also sort me a gig at the Telluride festival. I knew I wasn't really bluegrass but fuck it. I was up for it and I guess they had some swing with the festival because in a matter of days the show was booked and the plan was set. Check me out. That shit was too good to be true.

And it really was.

I was in Frank's bus en route to the festival when I got a text from Winston from Mumford and Sons - Ted was unwell. It was very serious and he'd been taken to hospital due to a blood clot on the brain. All shows were cancelled. Of course, Ted's health was the only thing that mattered. I'm very pleased to tell you that it was all sorted. He was on the mend and back on stage in a matter of months. At the time, though, it was very scary. The band, the festival, everything could wait - and little old me catching a ride? Well, that must have been very far down the list. I'm amazed I even got a text. But I did and it did leave me in a bit of a pickle.

I'm normally one to pack light, but this trip I had a large bag, my computer and my guitar in a hard case. I couldn't leave anything on Frank's bus as they were all off to Europe. I could carry it all on foot but only just, and it certainly wasn't comfortable. I got my guest wristband, watched Frank's show, and then bid them (and the comfort of the bus) goodbye.

As you've probably gathered by now, this sort of shit happens to me a lot so I wasn't phased by it at all. I was actually in very high spirits. I had the gig at Bonnaroo and I'd just have to blag somewhere to sleep for a few nights. Oh, and somewhere to leave my stuff. As far as I was aware, my show in Colorado was still happening the following weekend. It was a mere fifteen hundred miles away. What's a twenty-four-hour drive? Maybe I could meet someone at the festival who'd be up for it? The alternative was that I'd simply ditch one bag and hitchhike. Sounded fucking great to me. I made my way over to the solar-powered stage and found a little spot underneath to put my bags and guitar. It looked safe enough so I left it and went and got stuck into the festival.

It was a great festival - very big, very colourful, very tidy, and it had an overall pay it forward - be nice attitude. It sort of felt like it was everyone's first festival, which is a very good thing. I made some friends, saw some great acts (including Kacey Musgraves for the first time - now one of my all-time favourite songwriters), got drunk on expensive beer, and then woke up underneath the stage I was playing on that day. I couldn't remember heading back or making that decision, but it was a wise one. It was a great place to kip and one that I'd be able to return to that night. Sorted.

I played a fun show on the Solar Stage and the team behind it were very accommodating. I thought I'd been super sneaky and that it had gone unnoticed that I slept underneath the stage, but they'd all seen me crawling out that morning. I must have been quite the sight. After my show, I hooked up with a group of young excitable Americans and went bouncing around the festival. After a while, I lost them so I went bouncing around by myself. At some point I was given an E. I'm not one hundred percent sure if I bought it or if it was given to me.

At the time, taking an E was about as normal as smoking a spliff or doing a shot of tequila, especially at a festival. Since my first ever E way back in 1998, they had always been close by. There was a time when I'd take them most weekends. Then, on occasions when one wouldn't do the trick, I'd happily neck a couple in one night. I'm not trying to show off but I want you to know that dropping a pill wasn't out of the ordinary. At all. I fucking loved them. I've had some beautiful, eye-opening experiences on ecstasy. I've felt I could express myself and my love for everything and everyone in a way that I still hold dear in my heart today. That night wasn't much different. It's blurry but when the E kicked in, I danced some, talked a lot, and bounced around. I made it back to my little spot underneath the stage soon after the sun came up. All pretty normal stuff really. Waking the next day, however, was not normal. It wasn't normal at all. I felt awful.

I'd been noticing my comedowns getting worse as I got older - and I'd had some bad ones in my time. But my body usually waited until I stopped partying. At the end of the festival or the tour, when I finally managed to get a few days of rest, that's when it would kick in. But not this time. This was different. I didn't feel physically ill or sick. It was a mental thing. I felt completely beat. I felt sad and when I addressed my current situation I felt alone and pretty much lost. With the comedown, I'd completely lost my confidence and with it went my sense of adventure. How the fuck was I going to get to a festival on a mountain in Colorado? What felt exciting the day before seemed impossible that morning. While contemplating all that, I was informed by the stage manager (who had seen me rise from underneath the stage again) that I wouldn't be able to sleep under the stage that evening. They closed the main area of the festival to the public on the Sunday night and they needed to take the stage down. I'd need to find somewhere else to sleep. Again, the mood had changed. The previous day it seemed fun and rock'n'roll to be sleeping under a stage. Today, I felt that I was in the way and I'd outstayed my welcome. He also informed me they were expecting a big storm and pointed to the big, black clouds that were gathering in the distance. They turned out to be carbon copies of the ones in my head. The ones that were clouding my judgement. I grabbed my shit and got out of there.

Two minutes of walking around the friendly, colourful festival and I knew I needed to leave. I needed to charge my phone and get on my computer. I needed to look at a map and work out what I was going to do. The idea of hitchhiking fifteen hundred miles was about the furthest thing from my mind. I didn't want an adventure. I wanted to go home.

The biggest difference between English and American festivals is cars. At Bonaroo, and at many US festivals I've been to since, I have been blown away by the fact that pretty much everyone drives their car onto the festival site. The campsites double as car parks. This is a stark contrast to the English way of parking miles outside of the festival and walking in with all your shit piled up in bags and trolleys. In the UK, that's a rite of passage for any discerning festival goer. The other option, of course, is public transport and shuttle buses. My plan was the latter. I'd get a shuttle bus to a train station, get myself to a hotel and make a plan. I wasn't even sure where I was - Tennessee is a huge state. I thought I was getting rides on tour buses in and out of the festival so I hadn't paid much attention. My new plan was to get to the gate, find a shuttle bus, and go wherever it took me.

The problem at the gate was that nobody knew what a shuttle bus was. Apparently, there were some buses going to and from the airport, but none running that day. There were some coaches but they'd gone and I would have had to book them in advance. I said to the wardens on the gate that I needed to leave the festival right now and get back to civilisation. I asked how would I do that. They explained the only way out was to get my car and drive. I could try and call a taxi but they didn't have a number. They also didn't have a phone and mine was long out of battery. When I enquired about where we were, and how far was it to the closest city, I was told it was a two-hour drive to Nashville.

I grew up listening to country music and always dreamed of going to Nashville. I pictured myself romantically walking in town, guitar on my back, a song in my head, and my heart on my sleeve. I'd be singing for the tip jar underneath the neon lights. Right then, I was a million miles away from that idealistic fantasy but only a couple of hours outside of Nashville in reality. I should have been excited but I wasn't. I was jittery and nervous. For a while, I just sat up against the fence staring into the distance not knowing what to do. That wasn't me. What the hell had happened to me? The more I thought about it, the worse it got. I was doing my own head in.

A few hours later, a coach pulled up at the gate and some clean, well-to-do looking festival goers got off and headed in. It must be a shuttle bus. I grabbed my stuff and just got on the bus. The driver called out that it was a hotel bus for hotel customers only. Yep. Yep. Sure. I was staying at the hotel. Whatever hotel it was, I was staying there. I promised. I sat myself down. No way was I getting off that bus. Luckily, the driver didn't question me any further and after about thirty minutes, two other people got on the bus and off we went. About an hour later we pulled up at a huge, plush hotel, seemingly still in the middle of nowhere. I booked a cab from the front desk, asking to be taken to the cheapest, closest hotel. After a short wait, and an expensive taxi ride, I found myself checking into a clean and comfy room at the Red Roof Inn, just outside Nashville airport.

Surely this was where the nightmare should have ended. I'd made it safely off site before the storm had hit, I was charging my phone, I had a solid wifi connection and I was in Nashville - an all-time dream of mine. But this wasn't the case. I still felt like shit. I couldn't give a shit about Nashville. I didn't want to see or talk to anyone, let alone wander into the city alone. I had a shower and I tried to sleep but it was impossible. The come down had me wired. It was like I was still on the E or that the E was still working but it was having the exact opposite effect of the night before. My mind was a sluggish mix of unjustified guilt and regret, a sense of hopelessness that I've never known before. I was staring into a well of sadness and the more I thought about it, the worse it got. I was going round and round in circles of thought with no clear end in sight.

I looked into travel to Colorado with the enthusiasm of a turnip. I had four days to get there but my options didn't look good. Flights were few and far between, expensive, and only went as far as Denver. I'd still have a five-hour drive up a mountain away from the festival. My cloudy, fragile mind made a decision and I did something that I never do. I pulled the show.

I then decided to book myself a flight home from Nashville. Something fucked up with my debit card, though, and it wouldn't book the flight. A long, expensive, and awkward conversation with the bank informed me that they had put a stop on my card because of bizarre activity. I kept failing on weird security questions they fired at me. When I did finally convince them that it was me trying to book a ticket and that I needed to get home, they said it could take up to forty-eight hours before my card would work again.

Yep. There was no 'could'. It pretty much took the full forty-eight hours. The longest forty-eight hours of my life. I finally managed to book the first available flight back. It was expensive and although I couldn't bear to do the maths, I was pretty sure it had eaten all, if not more, of the profits that I'd made on the whole tour. I spent another night on lockdown in my hotel room going over the facts...

Mumford and Sons had sorted me a show at a bluegrass festival in the Colorado mountains. I'd cancelled. I'd spent three days in a hotel just outside of one of my dream cities and had barely managed to leave the room. I'd been on tour for a month and was about to return home in the red. I didn't feel very proud of myself. When asking myself what the fuck had happened again, I realised it was that fucking E! If I hadn't have taken the pill, I would probably be halfway to Colorado with a new bunch of friends, singing songs and having fun. Even if I hadn't made it to the festival, I'd be in a Nashville honky tonk living out my lifelong dream. I wouldn't be staring at the clock, counting down the hours in a cheap motel, wishing I was at home. But, that's what I did.

By the time I did get back, the clouds had cleared. Lizzy had known from my bizarre phone calls that something was up, especially when I got home from tour early. That's something that never happens. A few days late, sure, but nearly a week early? She knew. I was ready to just sweep it under the carpet, though. I had a bad comedown and came home early. In a nutshell, that was all that had happened.

The next week we left for Glastonbury and although I didn't actually plan it, the strangest thing happened. I did the whole weekend without taking any drugs. Well, nearly. I got to late Sunday night when a friend handed me a gram of coke. I'd bought it a few weeks back but we'd lost each other. How or why she'd kept it so long confused me. No one has any drugs left on Sunday night at a festival. A gram of coke on Sunday night at Glastonbury is like gold dust.

Although I hadn't made a big thing of it, or mentioned it to anyone, I was kind of proud of myself for doing the weekend without a chemical high. I had shit loads of shows over the weekend and Lizzy and I were physically running from stage to stage. It was an incredible weekend but the few times any pills or coke were offered, I passed up on it and I didn't actively look for any. I still had a great time and played some great shows. I figured I'd done well and clearly that's why this gram had turned up out of nowhere - it was a reward. Fuck it. I did a line. I still had one more show. I was playing a few songs with my good friends Slamboree. They are a dream festival band that mix rave, circus and song. Playing with them is always a blast. We all smashed the gram of coke and then smashed the closing gig of the Bimble Inn tent. As I bent down to snort the last line, I was overcome with doubt. Did I really want a line? Did I need one? Never before in all my years had this ever happened. It was odd. I went against the questions in my head, though, and up my nose the line went.

The coke, as always, wore off pretty quickly, and being Sunday night there was no way of getting any more. My usual Glasto Monday morning tradition is to head up to the stone circle for the sunrise, but the coke wore off. I was beat. It had been a great weekend but now I just wanted to head back to the tent. Could it be the clouds returning?

Lizzy and I were camped behind Billy Bragg's Leftfield stage. It's a sweet spot and slap bang in the middle of the festival and we had our bell tent, too. We clambered in and Lizzy fell quickly to sleep. I, however, couldn't sleep. I lay there totally awake. I could feel the clouds coming in as I stared at the ceiling of the tent. I was staring at it all night long and into the morning, just battling off those clouds. I mulled over many things that night - who I was, what I wanted, and where I was going. I thought about how lucky I was to be doing what I do, to be there at Glastonbury after playing so many great shows. I'd just toured the USA. I'd just got a tip of the hat from Billy Bragg. That was what I'd dreamed of as a sixteen-year-old. That shit was happening. But so was something else. The drugs weren't doing what they used to do and, then, as the sun rose that morning, the worry became physical - a lump appeared in my throat.

In the bell tent that night, I had an epiphany of sorts. But in order for you to understand it fully, I need to explain another story. One that had been running alongside this one. The story of my fucked-up voice.

At that point in my life, my voice was a wreck. But it was also kind of my thing - my gimmick, if you will. Reviews of my albums would always be saying stuff like "gravelled croaks" or "battered sandpaper voice" and let's be honest, they were right. It was really fucked-up. I sounded like Beetlejuice but worse. Everyone I knew could do an impression of me. When I met new people, and first opened my mouth, I could see their shock and bemusement. It was bizarre and unnatural. That said, it was never a problem, quite the opposite in fact. I met lots of ladies that found it quite the turn on. Talking to people I didn't know on the phone was great as people presumed they were talking to some kind of monster and would do whatever I asked. And when it came to my music, well my voice was a sure-fire sign that I was telling the truth. The voice was a symbol of every party, every cigarette, every line, every cheer and every late night conversation held in front of a massive speaker at full volume. These were the things I was singing about and my fucked up voice was the proof that I meant them. However, it was getting worse. Fast. It had been getting worse since I first started smoking. It worsened again when I switched to roll-ups without filters. The fags beat it down, the coke cut it up, and the long E chats would batter it some more. After a heavy weekend, there would be songs in my set that I wouldn't be able to sing because of the register and that list kept getting longer. At a time when I was getting more and more gigs, my voice was getting lower and lower, and that night in the bell tent it hit the bottom.

When I say I had a lump in my throat, I'm not talking metaphorically, as if I was nervous about something. I'm talking an actual lump. It felt like it was about the size of a egg. It grew to that size over the course of the morning while I was staring at the ceiling of the bell tent contemplating my life and battling my new found comedown demons. By the time Lizzy woke, I couldn't talk. I could barely get a croak out and when I did, it hurt. I realised I was in trouble. Lizzy could see it and we headed straight to the car. Lizzy drove us both back. I was silent. Physically, I had to stay silent but I did manage to get few words out. I said "I think I may be done with the drugs."

If I had the ability to talk, I would have gone into more detail and explained how I felt the night before after the line of coke. Or how the E had made me feel when I was in the States. Or I would have explained that if my voice kept getting worse, I wouldn't be able to talk anymore, let alone sing. I thought about how I'd be a fool to squander all the amazing opportunities that were presenting themselves to me. I'd kind of come around to the fact that the drugs weren't going to get any better. I'd been there and I'd done them. I'd loved, laughed, snorted, dropped and smoked my fair share. I'd enjoyed every minute but if I wasn't having fun, what was the fucking point? I kept those thoughts to myself, though. At the time, I thought I might wake up the next day and completely change my mind.

The next day the lump felt bigger and the pain when I talked got worse. I figured I needed to see a doctor. The whole twelve or so years I'd been living in London, I'd never once needed a doctor. A few trips to A&E? Yes. But never a doctor. I knew that because I hadn't registered with a doctor, nor did I know my NHS number - none of the things you needed to be seen. Obviously, this slowed the process of getting an appointment. I had to jump through some hoops and it took me a few days, but I got an appointment in the end. Over those days, I pictured how the conversation with the doctor would go. I'd tell them my voice had been deteriorating slowly for years, constantly getting worse. I'd tell them I smoked upwards of twenty rollies a day and did cocaine upwards of three nights a week. I'd tell them I spend weekends on long benders, talking loudly in noisy environments. Oh, and that I was a singer with a summer full of festival shows coming up - starting that very weekend, nonetheless. At that point, they were probably going to tell me that I had cancer. At least that's what it felt like at the time. This lump. Who would be surprised if it was?

It wasn't. Thank fuck.

I'd not smoked or snorted since returning from Glastonbury, right up until I saw the doctor. In return, the lump had gone down and my voice was sounding better. Even after just three days of not smoking, I could physically feel the difference. I knew what I had to do. I had to stop, right then and forever - fags, coke, pills, K, speed, acid... the lot. Okay, not weed. I'll never stop smoking weed but that's different. Oh, and booze. I didn't count that either. But cigarettes and chemical drugs, that was the box I drew. I'd actually made this decision in the bell tent that night and hadn't touched anything since, but now it was clear. That was it. I was drawing a line. The doctor agreed that was the best course of action. But as I said, my mind was made up and it felt good.

The following weekend would be my first festival as the new me. It was Blissfields, a festival I'd been playing for years. I knew the organisers and regulars like family. We are family, in fact. On top of that, my actual family came along. Well, my Mum and Dad at least. It had been six days since I'd smoked a cigarette and not only had the lump disappeared, but my voice actually felt and sounded better than it had in years. In six days! Nobody who watched the show would have noticed a change in my voice, but for me the difference in that gig was huge. I felt more in control of how I was singing than ever before. I didn't have to skip any songs and I could put more into it than any show I could remember. It was an incredible feeling.

Up until the show, I'd kept my epiphany to myself. Lizzy knew what was going down of course, but I'd not mentioned it to my folks or any friends. But after the show that night, I made it clear I'd given up drugs. I told everyone about my epiphany and that I was a changed man. I'm not sure if anyone believed me or not, but to be honest, I didn't care. I knew and it was about me, not anyone else.

Driving home from Blissfields I felt great - a bit of a hangover but not a comedown. There wasn't a cloud in sight and no lump my throat. The opposite in fact. Over the course of the next month, my voice got clearer and clearer. It had taken me around fifteen years to get it to the very bottom tones, but it was coming back up a lot faster. It was healing quicker than I would ever have imagined. The summer flew by and I was playing some of the best shows I ever had, more opportunities were arising and although people all around me were still racking lines and dropping pills, somehow they vanished from my view. I stopped wanting them and with that they seemed to disappear from my sight. My choice was clear. I could either take drugs and smoke cigarettes or I could continue to sing. I chose the latter and haven't smoked one cigarette or touched any chemical drugs since. No regrets.

INTERVAL
A PARTY OF PIZZAS

This interval isn't a story. I'm not actually sure what it is, but it's something that I want to publish with the hope of adding a new string to the bow of the English Language.

At a beautiful wedding on the Devonshire coast a few years ago, Lizzy and I were sat at a table with some friends of ours, Thom and Anna Stone. Somewhere in the conversation, we got to talking about collective nouns.

A murder of crows, a gaggle of geese, a melody of butterflies. So poetic and so en pointe. Who, we wondered, actually came up with all of these?

We then released that not everything has a collective noun. Fruit and vegetables, for example. We realised that they didn't have collective nouns. Therefore, we did the only reasonable thing we could think of and spent the rest of the afternoon coming up with collective nouns for all the fruit and veg we could muster up.

It's an honour to share them here with you now. By publishing them here in this book, I'd like to formally introduce them all to the English Language.

If you feel we've missed anything, please do get in touch with suggestions and I'll run them past the 'Committee of Collective Nouns for Fruit and Vegetables'. That committee consists of myself, Lizzy, Thom and Anna Stone.

Please use them as much as possible and spread the word.
Enjoy...

A sunshine of coconuts
A parade of pineapples
A team of tomatoes
An arse of peaches
A darkness of carrots (planted)
A vision of carrots (uprooted)
A rabble of radishes
A bunch of bananas
A table of lemons
A tequila of limes
A stomping of grapes
A harvey of potatoes
A system of oranges
A mystery of lettuce
An orgy of passionfruit
A forest of asparagus
A spasm of cucumber
A shitstorm of strawberries
A flute of figs
An assembly of apples
A fellowship of pears
A grasp of melons
A fart of raspberries
A wound of grapefruits
A fumble of pomegranates
A pattern of watermelons
A haka of kiwis
A cunt of papaya
A harem of mangos

An antelope of cantaloupe
A bully of gooseberries
A battalion of aubergine
A religion of artichokes
An idiot of parsnips (planted)
A tradition of parsnips (uprooted)
A street of corn
A trip of mushrooms
A sensation of broccoli
A tampon of garlic
A chippendale of olives
A cry of onions
A shirley of leeks
A whisper of wheatgrass
A quest of beetroot
A confusion of arugula
A flame of bok choi
A calorie of celery
A pepper of peppers
A rhyme of oranges
A halloween of pumpkins
A whimper of shallots
A steamer of kale
A gnarl of ginger
A christmas of sprouts
A squirrel of nuts
A kaleidoscope of cauliflower
A wrinkle of nectarines
A friendship of peas
A declaration of apricots
A wash of seaweed
A blister of cherries

GET YOUR DICK OUT

Most of these stories are set back in the day so I forgive you for thinking that the random days and wild nights are behind me - that now I'm living the clean life overlooking a river and writing a book. That is not the case. As mentioned, most of this book has been written on a train as I travel solo around Germany for my first proper headline tour of mainland Europe. I've completely fallen in love with the country. I came out two days after our evil headmistress, Theresa May, triggered 'Article 50', putting in motion England's departure from the EU. In light of this, it felt like a good time to start making bonds. My trip out here has been a wild one. There's been brilliantly bizarre shows, some dancing around the language barrier, Hip Hop videos, house concerts, and more beer than I've ever tackled in a ten-day stint. So, in many ways the book is still being written.

These days I do around thirty festivals a summer. I'm now the proud owner of a full UK driving license and an even prouder owner of a van called Bongo. We can leg it up and down the country, do a festival show, sleep in the van and then move off to another show the next day. When I say 'we' I mean me, Bobby Banjo and my beautiful wife, Lizzy Bee (who I've purposefully not written about much in this book - some stuff should stay private and if you want to know more about her, listen to one of the many love songs I've written about her).

However, at the end of the summer of 2016, during the August bank holiday weekend, both Lizzy and Bob had a friend's wedding that they wanted to attend. One of the few downsides of what I do (and there really aren't many) is that I miss a lot of weddings. People generally get married on summer weekends which is when I'm out and about doing my thing. If I've missed your wedding, sorry! So Lizzy and Bob were going go to the wedding and I was going to do the festival shows I had booked. I had Shambala in Northampton and Victorious in Portsmouth. I was going to do them alone. It sounded like fun. I've been to plenty of festivals by myself although I'd never had to drive between them before. Yes, I can legally drive but I'm not a particularly great driver, especially after a big night out. I guessed that I'd just have to avoid going too crazy at Shambala and be fit to drive to Pompey on Sunday morning. No worries.

I'd never been to Shambala before but I had heard wonderful things, especially from within the festival community. Festival legend and all-round hero, Chris Tofu, told me it was "the festival workers' festival". He and most other people I spoke to were surprised I'd never played as everything about it sounded right up my alley. I was playing early afternoon on the Saturday, opening up the main stage. I decided to head down Friday night and get stuck in. That would also be my last weekend of gigs before I went off to record 'A Spanner In The Works' so I had a bunch of new tunes banging around in my head. I thought maybe I'd be able to pick up some gigs in 'Coyote Moon Cafe' or some other tea tents and shisha bars around the site. That would mean I could test-run a few tunes that I hadn't played live yet.

The rumours were true. Shambala is a truly beautiful event. A forward thinking, colourful, environmentally-minded party with a strong eclectic lineup of top quality music from all around the world. It was quite odd going in by myself. I'm not really one for farting around and since I was in the van, I didn't need to pitch a tent or actually do anything on arrival. I parked the van and went straight to the bar. Once there, I wasn't alone at all. There were plenty of friends old and new. I arranged a couple of little unannounced shows for later that evening and got stuck into the party. It was a top night of dancing, drinking, talking, smoking and general festival tomfoolery. I played a few gigs that I don't remember (people informed me about them later) and I woke up in the van with a few hours to spare before showtime. Straight back to the bar then.

It was a sunny morning and if you're playing an outside, main stage slot, that is a huge fucking blessing. A nice crowd turned out for the show and sat down around the field. Perfect. I was in that kind of a mood and I took to the stage. The show was going well. I was doing my thing. It was all smiles. I'm sure it won't come as a surprise to you but I love being on stage - any shape, any size, any place. If I'm allowed, I'll get up. I feel comfortable up there. I feel honest and I've played so many gigs that a Beans on Toast show is the most natural thing in the world for me. I actually find a lot of similarities between being on stage and having sex. There's something about the mindset that is similar. What I mean is that you can fully concentrate on the main event but at the same time, your mind can drift between other thoughts and feelings. I love having sex. Anyway, let's not go there - I'm off track.

Shambala. Saturday afternoon. Sunny, smiley crowd. About half way through the set, I noticed a chap in the audience that was really enjoying it. In fact, maybe he was enjoying it too much - something that's actually hard to do, even for a sit-down crowd. He would start clapping then he'd sort of ball up his hands and cheer, but the cheer was verging on a scream. I cracked on with another song making a mental note to keep an eye on him. At the end of the next song, he started pulling up grass with his hands and actually screaming. He was smiling but it was a manic smile, and by the end of the next song he was up on his feet shouting random words while clapping and, you guessed it, screaming. I knew exactly what was happening. He was tripping and it was going the wrong way. Fast. The chap needed some help. He needed to snap out of it. By this time, pretty much the whole crowd knew what was going on as well. I was going to have to intervene. I knew that once I'd addressed the situation that the attention of the whole crowd was definitely going be on him. Now, that's probably not ideal if you're trying to guide yourself out of a bad trip. But, I figured he was already doing a good job of getting the attention anyhow, and I had to do something.

I've had a few bad trips but that doesn't make me any more clued up on how to talk someone down from one. I just went in with "Hey man, you okay?" and suggested he calm down. It had the opposite effect and he started going berserk. "Give him a tray" I shouted into the mic. Now, that obviously sounds like a fucking stupid thing to say. It made sense to me at the time, though. This, Ladies and Gentlemen, is the wisdom of Bobby Banjo. He insists that a tray will level any situation. Everyone is equal when holding a tray. They look like a bit of an idiot and their hands are out of action. I've seen trays level bizarre situations in the past and thought it might work here. Of course, there were no trays in sight and nobody knew what on earth I was on about. I hadn't thought it through properly. Now the guy was going apeshit, screaming and shouting at the top of his voice. He still had a huge manic smile. I needed another plan.

I shouted "GET YOUR DICK OUT!"

I guess I thought that one through even less! I was thinking that the thought of public nudity might shock some sense into the guy. I've never seen this course of action work in the past but I'd already said it so it was too late. Obviously, that didn't do any good either. Something strange did happen, though. Out the corner of my eye, I saw someone who was dressed as a policeman get his dick out. Things were getting weird.

Thankfully, somebody finally came to the assistance of the manic, tripping guy. It was somebody that was professionally trained, or at least better at dealing with the situation than I was. He was kind of politely ushered away to the welfare tent (I followed it up with them later and they said that it had been a bad trip. They'd provided a bit of peace and quiet and a cup of tea, and the lad was all good).

The gig went back to normal. It was a very enjoyable show. In fact, I can remember trying to book myself to open the stage every year. That's not how it works, unfortunately. You can't book yourself festival shows - they have to book you. Hopefully, Shambala will invite me back one some time. I knew I had to get to Pompey the following day. Easy. I'd just start drinking heavily then and there to ensure I was in bed at a reasonable hour. I cracked on with that promptly. I kept my guitar on me and rolled around the festival, playing a few tunes and high fiving folk. I bumped into loads of people - either old friends, or people that had enjoyed the show, would stop me for a little chat and then I'd move on. I was having a ball.

Early evening I nipped backstage to grab a beer and I walked past the onsite cash office. That's where bands go to get paid. I was hammered by this point and was continuing my day of saying idiotic things. So, I stuck my head in and said "Gimme all your money!" and made little guns out of my fingers and thumbs. These days show fees are wired directly into my bank account. If they're being picked up in cash, then Bob does it. So, I had no idea I was supposed to pick up any cash. When I say no idea, my booking agent, Adam, had given me a piece of paper with all the information on it. This included the cash collection but either I hadn't looked at it, or I'd forgotten. Either way, I only did the "gimme your money thing" as a stupid joke because I saw the cash office sign. I was expecting to be told to go away but one of the three pretty girls inside said "Beans, there you are - we've been waiting for you." Really? I thought. Oh, okay. I stepped into the office. They said I was the last one to be paid. I just needed to sign for the envelope and then the three of them were done for the day. I signed for the cash.

Now, I don't want be crass, or get into how much I get paid to play festivals, but I can tell you that it varies. I played for many years for next to nothing and I'm lucky to have Adam to do the negotiating for me (thanks, man!) so let's just say it was a wedge of cash. Getting paid to do something you love is a wonderful feeling. It can also have the effect of believing the money isn't real (even if you've got very real bills at home). In addition to this, I often get taken by a feeling of easy come, easy go. I manifest this into a character I call the Milkybar Kid - as in 'the Milkybars are on me'. In this analogy the Milkybars are drinks and I'm getting the rounds in.

Thinking about it now, I think my Milkybar Kid was invented a few years before at The Fleece in Bristol. We'd sold the venue out. That was a first for me at a venue of that size and since it was sold out, the promoter said he could settle up before the show. I was already pissed. Like I said, Bob normally settles up after the show but he was busy setting the stage up, so I said I'd settle up. He gave me over one thousand pounds. What the fuck? I could remember playing shows for fifty quid. Shit, I must have played hundreds for free. I knew the fees were getting better but, at the time, I thought it was crazy. I walked up on stage and before singing any songs, I said "I'm getting paid a grand for this gig, Folks. Let's make it fucking great."

Over the course of the gig, I brought up the cash thing again and made a deal with the crowd. It didn't seem right getting that much money for having that much fun. So, I suggested that everybody at the show was invited for a night out in Bristol afterwards. On me. Let's see if we can blow a grand out on the town. Fuck it. I remember saying. And that's what we did. There was about forty people that hung around until we were all packed up (actually forty-six because I remember ordering forty-six jagerbombs at the first club we hit), and we went into town looking for Big Jeff (a whole different story). I bought massive rounds and paid for everyone to get into a few clubs. I came around on the dancefloor at Mr Wolfs surrounded by people in Beans on Toast t-shirts. I'd blacked out for a bit. Maybe I'd blown the grand? I bid them farewell. Once I was back at my friends, Bob informed me that he'd actually got the money off me and sent me off with three hundred quid in my pocket. Fifty pounds of it was still there so I'd only spent two hundred and fifty. I'm not sure if the folks who came out thought we'd spent a grand. I guess it doesn't matter. It was a fun night even if we didn't find Big Jeff.

Anyway, back to this story.

I signed for the cash and instantly turned into the Milkybar Kid. "If you three girls have been in here all day, and now your finished, can I buy you a drink? I think you deserve it and you know I'm good for it." I held up my envelope. I'm tempted to bend the truth here and say that they packed up, locked up the office, and came straight to the bar. But that didn't happen. They did take me up on the offer but said for me to go ahead they'd come and find me a bit later. Not to worry, though, as the Milkybar Kid has never had much trouble finding friends.

At this point, the story goes a bit blurry and I'm not sure if the game I invented was with the girls from the cash office or some new friends I'd found on my travels. Either way, I was with three, new female friends, hanging out, getting hammered and enjoying the late night delights of the festival. We were at a bar talking about my set earlier. I was trying to explain the reasoning behind shouting "GET YOUR DICK OUT!" to the guy who was tripping. You can see above that it's pretty crap reasoning and I doubt I was explaining myself any better that time around. I was mid-story when a chap walked over to join our conversation. Me, being riddled with alcohol and general nonsense, looked at him and said "GET YOUR DICK OUT!"

Without missing a beat, the guy got it out. He didn't wave it around or anything but the whole thing came out for a full second and then went back into hiding. I couldn't believe it. I'm not sure why but that was the last thing I thought was going to happen. Everybody cracked up laughing, including the guy who'd just got it out (obviously a very self-confident man). Surely it's not supposed to be that easy, I thought. I leant over to a guy standing in a nearby group "Oi, mate, GET YOUR DICK OUT!" Boom. Out it came. It was crazy and absolutely hilarious. The Milkybar Kid got another round in and the game was born.

I saw nineteen dicks that night. I'd say I had a seventy percent success rate and mostly without needing any kind of encouragement. I only stopped at nineteen because somewhere along the way it was decided that if I got to see twenty, then I should get mine out - double standards I know, but I didn't fancy that. What was even crazier was that the three girls I was with couldn't convince anyone to get it out there and then (a few private showings were offered). With hindsight I appreciate that is sounds very foolish, but I am a fool - and it made for a fucking hilarious night. It wasn't a sexual thing. We were just having a laugh. It was a bunch of people having fun, being comfortable with their own bodies, and quite literally dicking around. I'm not sure if it was the festival, or if it was a full-moon or something, but I've not encountered a scenario since where that game seemed appropriate. At least I've not wanted to play it, anyway.

I've no idea how the night or game ended (which sounds dodgy, but I'm a trustworthy and faithful man - even when I'm the Milkybar kid). I just remember waking up late and having to drive to Pompey.

Victorious festival is very different from Shambala. It is also a wonderful event. It's set on the seafront in Portsmouth. There's no camping as it's right in town and it's fucking huge. Huge and affordable. A big problem with UK festivals is the ticket price. Not many people can afford to spunk a few hundred quid on a weekend before even setting off. Early Bird day tickets for Victorious are twenty pounds and only go up to around thirty. That's incredible, especially when they get the lineups they do. That year's headliners were Noel Gallagher, Calvin Harris and Natty. It was incredible for everyone who bought a ticket. However, it was a fucking nightmare for me. I was added to the bill last minute and barely made the printed programme. Those who did see it would notice that I was actually going be clashing with both Noel and Calvin that night.

Victorious is a very mainstream festival. Whereas Shambala is bohemian and world musicy, Victorious is indie and beer drinkery. Luckily, I fit into both camps, and feel comfortable at both, but who the hell was going to come and watch me when I was playing up against one of the world's favourite songwriters and one of the world's favourite DJs? The stage I was playing wasn't massive but it certainly wasn't tiny. Hey ho. I was there - I'd survived the drive, had a room at a nearby hotel, and it was my last show of the summer. I parked up…and went to the bar.

It was very easy to top up on the previous two days of drinking at Shambala and before I knew it, I was smashed - don't know what time it is kind of smashed. I was also cold as I'd forgotten to take my jacket from the van. I headed over to the stage to introduce myself. I got there just as the the act before me was finishing. In my drunken state, I managed to persuade the stage manager that it was a good idea for me to go on thirty minutes early. I was convinced that everyone would be watching Noel, or dancing to Calvin, but there was a fair few people kicking around. I presumed that they were still there from watching the previous act. Going on stage early at festivals is just not a done thing. Bands go on late, for sure. Accidents happen, things run overrun, that's life. But early? People just don't do it. I do, though. Why the fuck not? Soundchecks are boring and I don't really need them. So, if I'm allocated a thirty-minute soundcheck/change over time, and then a forty-five-minute set, I'll generally just get up and get cracking if the moods takes me. And yep, that day it definitely took me. The stage crew were confused by the idea but happy to go along with it. At some point along the way, I'd put on a high vis security jacket. I still have no idea exactly where it came from but I was no longer cold and looked legitimately like a security guard. I figured that it would be a fun start. So, thirty-minutes early, dressed like security guard, I bounded onto the stage, straight up to the mic and out of nowhere I shouted "GET YOUR DICK OUT!"

The crowd went wild.

Okay, maybe not wild but there was a decent size crowd and they definitely cheered. That meant they must have come for a Beans on Toast show. No way in the world was a crowd going to cheer at some random dude shouting that. I made a few Noel and Calvin jokes and asked the crowd if they minded if I started half-an-hour early. They cheered again. Yes! It was going be a great show. And then BANG! A security guard jumped on the stage and jumped on me. It turned out that I was wearing his jacket. I hadn't borrowed it at all. I'd stolen it.

Apparently, I wasn't being funny. I was impersonating an officer. I thought he was trying to get me off stage because I'd gone on early. It got very weird and confrontational. I realised what was going on and I gave the jacket back and apologised. Things calmed down but it was a very odd start to a show that was only going to get odder. The crowd were still there, though. More of them had arrived, in fact. Maybe they didn't know Noel was playing. I did a couple of tunes and in between them continued to shout "GET YOUR DICK OUT!" Telling in-jokes on stage isn't a great idea. Sometimes it's okay to tell jokes that only people on the tour will get. Bob and I will often do it to each other on stage - it can be very funny. But an in-joke that only I'm in on sounds like a stupid idea. Never one to shy away from laughing at my own jokes, I thought I was hilarious and knew that my new found friends back at Shambala would have thought so, too.

The show continued. It was nearing the end and I was about to do a song called 'The Chicken Song'. It's a song about the murderous horror of chicken farming. Then I remembered an email I'd received a few days before. People quite often email me asking for song requests or shout outs. It's really nice to get the emails, and I wish that I could tell you that I take the time to reply and then remember to dedicate particular songs to particular people, but the truth is, I don't. I have a hard time remembering the names of my friends, let alone people I've not met. When I'm doing a gig, I've got other shit going on in my head - especially that gig. It was the end of a banger of a weekend. However, for some reason, this one email came back to me just as I was about to do the tune.

This was the email:

Looking forward to seeing you at Victorious Festival on Sunday. I'm bringing my two boys with me; I've corrupted them young, introducing them to your stuff via Frank Turner and they are now two of your smallest (at 9 & 12), but biggest fans. I've told them I'll ignore when they sing along to the swearing so they are doubly made up.

I'm sure you already have things planned for the night but if you can squeeze it in, they'd both love the chance to see you do the Chicken Song. And if you could spare a second to say hi to Finn and Riley at some point during your set, they would probably see fit to send me to a much nicer nursing home when the time comes.

Kids at my gigs is a funny one. At actual gigs there's normally an age restriction initiated by the venue so I don't have to think about it. Festivals, though, they're are a different matter. I understand it's not children's music but I'm happy to play for kids. If open-minded parents want to bring kids along, I'm all for it. But then again, I'm not normally shouting about dicks.

I remembered the general request from the email but had no idea of the names. I just said "I'm going play 'The Chicken Song. Apparently there are some young kids out there that wanna hear it. If you're out there, guys, get up here on stage and you can do the chicken dance."

Seconds later two kids were passed over the crowd barrier and scrambled up onto the stage. So, I then said "In fact, any kids out there are welcome up on the stage if you want?" Children started flying over the barrier at an alarming rate. It felt like hundreds but it was probably more like ten to fifteen - still, very unexpected. Who knew there were so many kids out there hiding in the crowd? They all got up on stage and after some quick instructions, they made chicken noises and danced around like chickens while I sung the song. It was brilliant. Wanting to keep the momentum up after the song, I launched straight into the next one. I started to play 'A Whole Lot of Loving'. That's a protest song about a spiritual revolution. Then out of the corner of my eye, I saw one of the kids confidently singing along. I pulled the mic stand down and presented it to the kid. I'm terrible at judging the age of kids but

I'll have a guess and say he was eight or nine years old. He totally went for it. He sang the whole song, word for word (profanity included), in tune, and with confidence. The crowd went wild. Rightly so. He introduced himself to the crowd as Lucas. Fearful of getting the limelight taken away, I took the mic back and cracked on with the last few songs of the set.

I told the kids they could hang around on stage and dance, which they did. I completely forgot they were there as they'd kind of naturally moved to the back of the stage. As I played the last song of the night, my mind wandered - what a weekend it had been! I was thinking back to my Shambala friends and was taken by the moment. I finished the last song and out of nowhere I decided to finish the game 'GET YOUR DICK OUT'. I spun my guitar off, put my hand down my trousers, and out it came - just for a second, just like the first guy in the bar the night before. That was number twenty. Safely back inside, I turned around and remembered I was on a stage surrounded by kids.

Whoops.

The night didn't finish there. It actually involved me working on a pulled pork stand and starting a mini food fight, a mini rave from my van in the hotel car park, a midnight dip in the sea, and the purchase of some fine hash and an ugly hawaiian shirt. But that's a story for another time.

Hungover to fuck and driving back the following day, I realised that on paper what I'd done was very, very wrong. It was going to be hard to explain that one, and the wrong kind of chinese whispers could probably stop me from playing at the brilliant Victorious again.

On my return home, I got another email.

Thank you so much. My boys are made up. My place in a great old people's home is secured and tonight will go down in

history. Lucas was not one of my two but a legend all the same. A great experience for us all.
Great show as always

Maybe they didn't see it!

AT LEAST I'VE GOT
BOTH MY HANDS

I was in a hammock when I got the call.

It was a proper hammock, as well. Strung up perfectly between two glorious palm trees that looked like they'd grown in that very place, for that very purpose. They produced coconuts. I knew this because I had one in my hand. I'd seen R2 run up the side of the tree about ten minutes ago - a big fucking palm tree, too. He just hugged the sides, slammed his feet on the trunk and flew up the tree like it was nothing. Then he plucked a coconut and skipped back down. But it wasn't over there. He then pulled out a machete, hacked off the sides, chopped off the top, and conjured a straw out of thin air. He popped it straight into the middle of the coconut and handed it to me with a warm and generous smile. It was like he was some sort of coconut wizard.

I'm sure his name wasn't actually R2 but that's what it sounded like, and I'm not sure how else to put it down on paper. I'd met R2 late the night before. Me and Alice, my girlfriend at the time, arrived on the back of a knackered moped. The driver had crammed both of us on the back. I was exhausted, jet lagged and in a half dream/half awake travel state. We'd been turned away by a long line of guest houses and hostels, and it was looking pretty bleak until we found R2. Booking in advance was suggested in Lonely Planet but "what do they know?" I mansplained to Alice on the flight over. She was keen to book whereas I wanted to "go with the flow". It turned out I was wrong and Lonely Planet was right. It was actually looking pretty hairy the night before but that didn't matter anymore. I was there, coconut in hand, in my hammock.

I was in India, Goa to be precise. If you really want to get to the nitty gritty, we were on a secluded beach in Patnem. It was my first time in the country and Alice and I were staying there for six weeks. The plan was not to have a plan. We were just going to travel around. Aiming to get away from it all, see some of a new country, soak up some sun, we wanted to live the easy life. Once we found R2, we'd booked three nights in a little hut on the beach in Patnem. It was simple and beautiful and cost less than five pounds a night - exactly what I was looking for. We had enough cash to survive on a budget and not a care in the world. It was a welcome break from the hustle and bustle of North London and we couldn't wait to explore new lands and search for new experiences. All I had taken was my guitar and a small bag of clothes. Traveling light. The sun was shining down on me as I lay back in the hammock and listened to the waves lapping at the shore and the tropical birds singing in the sky. It was bliss.

Then the phone rang.

I didn't even know why I had my phone on me. I was surprised it even worked. Who knew you got signal in paradise? My phone was one of the things I was hoping to get away from but there it was. The all too familiar retro telephone ringtone was trying (unsuccessfully) to join in the dawn chorus. It was Ally. He knew full well where I was so I was surprised that he was calling. My mind drifted back to Holloway Road where I'd set off from forty-eight hours prior. It was dark, wet and freezing cold, and it was mid-December. Initially, I wasn't going to take the call. What did Ally want? I was on holiday. Then I started to think that I

113

wanted to tell Ally about the beautiful hut, and the beach, maybe even let him hear the birdsong. I'm not usually one to brag about being on holiday to those at home but he could take it. Fuck it. I answered the call. I immediately regretted it as Ally sounded super fucking stressed.

"JAY, WHAT THE FUCK? JAY...?"

I answered back but he couldn't seem to hear me.

"JAY...? ARE YOU THERE...? THE PUB'S ON FIRE... THE PUB'S ON..."

And with that, the line went dead.

My first reaction was to call straight back. Nothing. No signal at all. I took the phone to R2 who explained that you don't get phone signal in paradise. Anyway, what did I want with my phone when I had the sea, the sand and the sunshine? I wanted to know what was going on! I was confused as the phone had just worked. I tried again. Nothing. I tried to text. Wouldn't send.

I wasn't sure what to think. Was it a joke? Some kind of prank? I clocked that the time in the UK was late. There was a good chance Ally was at a party. What did he mean by fire? Where? How? There wasn't a huge amount I could do even if there was a fire. I was on the other side of the world. Maybe I'd misheard him. Yeah, I'd probably misheard him. Either way, I was sure it was nothing to worry about. So I did the only thing I could think of. I pretended that the call didn't happen. I climbed back into the hammock, picked up the coconut, and listened to the birdsong. It sounded different, though. Something had changed.

I decided against telling Alice about the call when she got up - no point in worrying her. We had some breakfast and went for a walk down the beach followed by a swim. Unfortunately, the phone call was never far from my mind. After lunch, I had to come clean to Alice. I told her it was probably nothing to worry about but I headed into central Patnem where I'd hopefully be able to pick up some signal. When the phone connected, the time in the UK would have been around 4am. I called Ally back but it went immediately to voicemail. The same thing happened with Stix, Danny and everyone else who lived at the pub. All voicemail.

The only thing I had to go on was a text.

Sorry to hear the news mate. Hope everything's ok.

It was from my friend, Mark, the drummer of Captain Black. I don't think he had ever sent me a text before. Sure, he drank at the pub but he didn't live there. What news was he on about? What the fuck was going on?

Hours passed without an answer. I sent a shit load of texts. I left voicemails. Nothing. I was in a strange state of limbo, waiting nervously for the retro telephone ringtone. When it finally pierced the silence, it was Ally again.

The pub had burnt down.

Ally didn't beat around the bush. Nobody was hurt. Everyone got out in time and was accounted for. That was the good news. There had been a fire, though. That was the bad news. It started in the basement. No fire alarms went off but the pub filled with smoke sometime after close. As usual a few people were hanging around for a bit of lock-in but they evacuated and sent word to those upstairs. Apparently, Andy Peyton had nearly died, refusing to believe there was a fire until he saw it with his own eyes. He eventually did, of course, but managed to make it down from the third floor all the same. Everyone had feared the worst for Sarah Crowder. She'd been staying in my room while I was away and nobody had seen her. It turned out that she just hadn't returned from her night out, though. They got her on the phone and she was okay. The pub, however, was not okay. "What about my room?" I enquired. That was on the top floor. Surely it was okay? Nope. It was gone. Everything was gone - The Holloways' equipment in the cellar, my computer, all the stuff in the office. Even all the artwork on my walls was gone. Up in smoke. The frame of the pub was standing but inside was a shell. A burnt out shell.

"Shall I come home?" I asked Ally.

"Jay, nobody here thinks you're ever gonna come home. There literally isn't a home to come back to."

Ally promised to let me know as and when there was more information. He quickly explained, though, that there could be no more information. The pub had burnt down. End of story.

Fortunately for all of us, that was not the end of our story. It was, in fact, the start. As far as this book is concerned, it's only the second chapter. The pub was, of course, Nambucca. My home for the previous five years. It was a home to eight of my closest friends and a home to hundreds of others over the years. For me it was also a source of income. That pub was my house and my job.

However, changes had been afoot there well before I'd left for my travels. The whole time we'd been there the pub's lease had been for sale. We knew that. It was just a case of nobody wanting it - hence we got away with doing as we pleased. But recently things had started to change. People with suits would come into the pub with clipboards and start pointing at things. There was even talk of paying rent. As I walked out the door, on my way to India, I'd actually said "Don't do anything rash while I'm away."

And then that happened.

At the time, I walked back towards the hut, my mind a jumble of thoughts and emotions. I was almost numb. Paying no attention to the blue sky, the birdsong, or the vastly different culture all around me, I thought about how I was going to break the news to Alice. A few weeks before we left, Alice had moved into the pub. Dave had moved out and we'd acquired his room as a living room and place for Alice to keep all her beautiful clothes. It was the first time she'd moved out from her folk's house. Now her clothes, and all the rest of her belongings, were gone, and it was down to me to tell her. Trying to put that off for as long as possible, I got back to our place and I went to see R2 . He was manning the little hut where you checked in.

"I've just found out that my house has burnt down back in London." I told him. "I just got the call. Everything I own is gone."

R2 looked at me, smiled and said "At least you've got both your hands."

Shit me. He was right. I looked down at both my hands and they were still there, fully functioning. For that I should be thankful. I was thankful. I still am thankful.

Hands down that was the best piece of advice I've ever received. From that very moment, I didn't shed one tear over any of the possessions I lost. After all, they were just possessions. That advice not only gave me the strength to talk to Alice, and console her, but it has given me strength ever since. It's actually formed a large part of my own personal philosophy. Even during tough times, especially during tough times, it's important for us to realise what we do have. We should count our blessings and hold them dear. I'd like to think that this shines through in my songs. Friends are important and all my friends were safe. Everything else? Well, that was just stuff. I'd find somewhere to live. I'd find work. I'd be alright. I'd use both my hands.

After talking to Alice, I caught a glimpse of my guitar. It was happily leant up against the wall in the corner of the hut. The one thing that I'd one hundred percent save from a burning building and I had it with me. That was a sign.

The next six weeks travelling India were beautiful. If you've not been, it's hard to describe. Usual rules don't apply. Everything is different and from that, I found an incredible peace. Many of the Indians I met lived by a similar philosophy to R2 and had a very similar smile. We saw some beautiful landscapes, sea, sun and the birdsong sounded better than ever. I also witnessed some extreme poverty which put my situation into harsh perspective and made me appreciate my life more than ever before. Fire or no fire, I was lucky.

While travelling round, Dave and I spoke regularly and put plans together for setting up something new on my return. I felt good. Really good. As cheesy and obvious as it sounds, I think I went to India to find myself and I achieved it. I'd found myself in a ball of flames on the other side of the world. Without knowing it, I think I was longing for a change and that's what I got.

A few days before we returned to London, I got an email from a friend. Alan Pownall is a mate and a great songwriter. He'd heard about the fire and at the time had an empty flat in Old Street. He'd rented it for a six month period but had to move out and still had two months left on the lease. Providing I'd leave it as I found it, he said that Alice and I could stay there. Absolute lifesaver. I knew that we would have places to stay on our return. Over the years so many different people had passed through Nambucca's doors, be it for the night, the week, or even moving in for a few months. We had a very open door policy so I had a few people I could call upon for somewhere to crash. Our own flat for two months rent free, though? Fuck, yes! Alan had never personally stayed at Nambucca. I'd never put him up as such but that's not how karma works. It has its own rules and for me, they were working just fine.

The next two months at Alan's house were spent head down, hard at work, setting up a new venue. We were taking over a venue in Kentish Town. It was to be called The Flowerpot. There were rooms upstairs and a stage downstairs. We'd made enough of an impact from our parties at Nambucca to get involved with some backers and folks who knew the trade.

At Alan's house, using both my hands and my saved guitar, I penned the last few tunes from my debut album. If I couldn't play every other night at Nambucca, I was going to need to get some gigs elsewhere. That's when I started booking myself more and more shows.

Fast forward ten years and here we are. I've played over a thousand shows since then - all over the world. At the time of writing, I'm just about to release my ninth album and you're holding my first book in your very hands. If you've got all this way, then thank you. Will anybody even read it? Who knows? Maybe it will go to shit and I'll just have boxes full of unread books in the corner of my room. It wouldn't surprise me. I am surprised I got this far. If that is the case, so be it. At least I've got both my hands.

AFTERTHOUGHTS

So, there you have it. I've just read through the final draft of my book and it'll be getting sent off to print next week. Nuts. Before it does, I thought I'd share some thoughts and thank yous.

All these stories are true and as far as I'm concerned, they actually happened. I've been telling them for years, either on stage, in song, or down the pub. Each time you tell a story it shapes itself, generally for the benefit of the story over the facts. That may well have happened here, but that's life.

I was telling my old man about the book at Christmas. When I told him that the opening chapter was the story of my first Glastonbury, he asked if I'd included the part where I rang home crying, saying I didn't have any money or anywhere to stay, and that I was wet, cold and wanted to come home. I don't remember that at all. I called bullshit but my Dad swears it's true. Maybe I've painted a prettier picture of myself. Even so, my Dad 'apparently' told me to sort myself out, head down to the festival and work it out. That's actually the story that you heard so thanks, Dad.

Also, now's a good time to thank the people I work with on this musical adventure. Adam Gainsborough, who alongside being a true friend and trustworthy sounding board, books my shows and helps me navigate the ship. Xtra Mile Recordings, who have

120

been releasing my music from album one and continue to be a pleasure to work with, and Lyndsay Davies for helping me with my poor grammar and spelling and bashing this book into shape.

Most of all, though, I'd like to thank you for taking the time out of your busy life to read a few stories from mine. Thanks for coming to the gigs, listening to the music and generally giving a shit. I wouldn't be able to do this without you and I fucking love doing this.

Beans x

www.beansontoastmusic.com